Ron Huntington

Strategic Business Planning

A Service of

NAHB

BuilderBooks™
National Association of Home Builders
1201 15th Street, NW
Washington, DC 20005-2800
www.builderbooks.com

Strategic Business Planning
Ron Huntington

ISBN 0-86718-548-1

Cover design by Armen Kojoyian
Printed in the United States of America
LOC data is available.

Disclaimer
This publication is designed to provide accurate and authoritative information in regard to the subject matter covered. It is sold with the understanding that the publisher is not engaged in rendering legal, accounting, or other professional service. If legal advice or other expert assistance is required, the services of a competent professional person should be sought.
—From a Declaration of Principles jointly adopted by a Committee of the American Bar Association and a Committee of Publishers and Associations.

For further information, please contact:
BuilderBooks™
National Association of Home Builders
1201 15th Street, NW
Washington, DC 20005-2800
(800) 223-2665
Check us out online at: www.builderbooks.com

03/03 SLR / Data Reproductions Corp., 2000

ABOUT THE AUTHOR

Ron Huntington is principal of his company, Executive Mentors & Trainers in Seattle, Washington, and a partner in Sound Investments, a pacific northwest real estate development company. As owner of Executive Mentors & Trainers (EMT), which specializes in general management and leadership skills development and business performance consulting services, Ron is both owner and a senior consultant to management with EMT. As a partner in Sound Investments, he oversees the company's business management activities and property development investments.

Ron has more than 30 years of entrepreneurial business development, ownership and general management experience, which includes start-ups, operations management, raising capital, investor relations, and financial stewardship. He received his bachelor's degree from the University of Washington with studies in Communications and Sociology. He is a professional member of the Society for Human Resource Management (SHRM), as well as the designated pacific northwest coach for the Gazelles/Masters of business dynamics program.

An accomplished public speaker, his strong facilitation background has served a varied and diversified group of clients, which includes National Association of Home Builders, McArthur Homes, The Jon Campbell Companies, Trammell Crow, Marvin Windows & Doors, Weyerhaeuser Realty Investors, Microsoft Corporation, Peoplesoft, AMMEX Corporation, Group Health Cooperative, Amdahl, The International Oracle User's Group of the Americas, The International Loss Adjusters Association, Intracorp, Unionbay Sportswear, MUZAK, The ARMCO Group, Western Steel, RC Services, Ford Motor Company Dealers, Mostly Muffins, Thales Avionics, The Safe Streets Alliance, and The Washington Family Council.

His consulting specialties and skills include general management, strategic and business planning, sales and marketing management, personal and professional financial planning, personal and professional coaching and mentoring, family-owned businesses, succession and transition planning, customer and client service programs, communications strategies, working and interpersonal relationships, conflict resolution, and human resources management.

ACKNOWLEDGMENTS AND DEDICATIONS

~ To Evie, my sweet bride, for patiently and supportively enduring my ten weeks in The Bunker, without complaint, while this book was under construction.

~ To Nick, my Eagle Scout and young Husky, for being a son any father would take pride in calling his own.

~ To my Dad, Clay Huntington, and my Mom, Jan Huntington, for all their unflinching support over the years—and who still cannot figure out *exactly* what I do and *precisely* how I earn my living.

~ To Theresa Minch and the people at BuilderBooks, for all their guidance and assistance along the way to: "It's a wrap!"

~ To Verne Harnish, at Gazelles, for the perpetual inspiration and the opportunity-laden introductions you provide.

~ To Lorne Zalesin, at Biltmore Homes, for initially hooking me up with the good folks at the NAHB, making this book possible.

~ To my own Mentors along the path of life—Don Wolvers, Rich Komen, Don Lusk—and to my two Pardners—Steve Smith and Saeed Abtahi—for all the Gifts you provided and may never have realized their full impact.

~ To Dave, Don, Ron, and Steve McArthur at McArthur Homes, for the opportunity to work with your fine family, and to help take you to the places where you can all live your dreams.

~ To my Sister, Cheryl Franco, for being the best Sister, traveling companion, and professional Parental Escort on the planet.

~ And lastly, to my Brother, Mark Huntington, who left us way too soon, before his full life's work was done.

BOOK PRODUCTION

Strategic Business Planning was produced under the general direction of Gerald Howard, NAHB Executive Vice President and CEO, in association with NAHB staff members Michael Shibley, Executive Vice President, Builder, Associate, and Affiliate Services; Greg French, Staff Vice President, Publications and Nondues Revenues; Eric Johnson, Publisher, BuilderBooks; Theresa Minch, Executive Editor; and Jenny Lambert, Assistant Editor.

CONTENTS

FIGURES

SECTION I
ASSESSMENT

1

THE STRATEGIC BUSINESS PLAN

"Nothing is inevitable, unless our inaction makes it so."

Ronald Reagan

Whenever I speak to a group of NAHB 20 Club members, or to groups of other business owners about strategic business planning, invariably one of the first questions posed to me is:

"Why do I need to have a business plan?"

A nervous silence often descends on the group, as they awkwardly await my reply. My answer, to the surprise of many in the room, is always the same: "Well . . . not everyone needs a business plan."

The truth is you may not want or need a Strategic Business Plan for your business. Many businesses have operated successfully for years without a formal business plan and have done just fine, in their leader's opinion.

The decision to develop a Strategic Business Plan is most often motivated by two major reasons.

1. You concluded that you need a Strategic Business Plan.

◆ You want to gain a greater level of control over the forces facing you and your organization.

◆ You may be frustrated with the results you and your leadership team are delivering.

◆ You may be eagerly looking for competitive advantages in the markets in which you operate and compete.

◆ You might be looking to stabilize the financial performance of your company and to build in predictable, dependable, and sustainable levels of profitable future financial performance.

◆ You may wish to attract a higher quality of player to your organization, to strengthen the organization's performance capabilities and prepare it for competitive growth.

◆ Most importantly, you may believe a Strategic Business Plan can help you communicate your ideas for the future of your organization, building hope, carrying a heightened credibility, intensity, and commitment to your employees and key leaders.

2. Someone else told you that you need a plan.

Usually, business owners or leaders decide they need a Strategic Business Plan because *someone else* tells them they need a plan. For example,

◆ The bank asks for a business plan before approving a new loan for a project or a business expansion.

◆ A potential partner needs a plan to determine whether he or she will join or invest in the business.

◆ Co-owners, or key leaders, say they need to provide confidence and help make better decisions in today's volatile economic and business environment.

Let's face it, developing a business plan because *someone else* suggests or demands that you do so imposes a burden or discomfort so overwhelming that it often stifles the desire to start the work. It can take some of the fun and motivation out of facing the wealth of opportunities that come with designing and building an effective Strategic Business Plan.

If you are a business owner, you are likely an entrepreneur, a taker of calculated risks. Self-motivated, you are used to setting your own direction, your own pace, your own rules, and your own limits. You see yourself as able to meet any challenge and survive any setback. During the past decade, you have grown accustomed to success, and it may have come to you rather easily.

Of course, many of you will admit that it has become more difficult to sustain your past levels of success. And, right now, you may be feeling more uneasy about the future, not knowing which way to move your business, protect your interests, safeguard your gains, and sustain your reputation. What will you do as you look to the future? Grow the business? Capitalize on the weaknesses of competitors? Scale back, to conserve and protect precious resources and conserve cash for future opportunities? What should you do? What will you do? What course, right now and looking into the future, makes the most sense for you and your business?

So we come back to your answering the pivotal questions posed earlier:

Why do *you* need a business plan?

Why are you considering designing and building a Strategic Business Plan *right now*?

As you consider your various reasons for building a Strategic Business Plan, keep in mind that the greatest beneficiary of this process is likely to be. . . . . you.

> *"If you don't design your own life plan, chances are you'll fall into someone else's plan. And guess what they have planned for you? Not much."*
>
> *Jim Rohn*

PURPOSE OF A STRATEGIC PLAN

Throughout any strategic business planning process there are three fundamental questions an organization must ask itself and answer:

1. Who and what are we today, what do we do now, and why?
2. What do we want to be and do in the future, and why?
3. How do we get from where we are today to where we want to be tomorrow?

> *"There is no security on this earth. Only opportunity."*
>
> *General Douglas McArthur*

An effectively designed and executed Strategic Business Plan is essentially a flight plan to your desired destination, defining points either along the way of your path or at your desired destination. An effective plan gets you from your current business concept and level of operating performance to your goal: a smarter, healthier, more successful business in the future. It gives you a clear picture of the obstacles that lie ahead and points out alternate routes for you to consider, particularly during those times when surprises inevitably occur.

There are multitudes of solid reasons for you to commit to embarking upon the strategic planning process. These reasons usually fall into three categories of consideration: strategic, operational, and financial.

STRATEGIC

◆ Attracting strategic business partners and alliances

◆ Ensuring that everyone in the organization is aligned and working toward the same goals and objectives

◆ Providing unified clarity in understanding the current realities of your organization and how they affect your ability to perform, regardless of market conditions

◆ Reducing stresses and tensions within the business over core philosophies, values, and direction

◆ In difficult times, having greater control over your destiny, with preordained options clearly spelled out and a positive outlook guiding your reactions

◆ Obtaining objective, truthful feedback and input from key leaders, employees, stakeholders, advisors, investors, or partners upon which to base decisions

◆ In the event a potential buyer courts your business, you have a prepared document to help you establish a higher value for the organization while building confidence in the value of an acquisition by all parties

OPERATIONAL

◆ Retaining key, skilled employees within your company

◆ Attracting key, skilled employees to your company

◆ Improving the quality of decision making within the organization in a more coherent, focused, confident, and coordinated manner while focusing your activities and optimizing the application of available resources

◆ Crystallizing your thoughts, best practices, and prudent policies in guiding and running the business

◆ Monitoring progress and making timely, effective course corrections when results differ from the plan in times of rapidly changing circumstances

◆ Improving communication and public relations, from a better measured and managed set of expectations, both inside and outside the organization

FINANCIAL

◆ Obtaining funding or receiving better, more favorable and competitive credit terms from key suppliers

◆ Understanding the full range of financial aspects, impacts, and considerations of your business, including critical cash flow and break-even requirements so that you do not run out of cash

◆ Managing growth and profitable performance with greater foresight and certainty

There are also a number of sound reasons *not* to take on the task of creating a Strategic Business Plan for your business, either right now or in the near future. Among the prudent reasons *not* to spend time wading through the strategic planning process are these:

◆ When the organization finds itself in a cash flow bind, no matter how severe, and must turn its full attention and energies to generating sales and gathering cash to remain solvent and viable. First things first: Stay in business!

◆ When there is a loss of key leadership or key performers who must first be replaced to regain positive equilibrium, momentum, or morale. Fill the vacancy with someone who can contribute significant value to the future development of the Strategic Business Plan when you resume the effort.

◆ If there is a less than total commitment from ownership or top leadership to fully support the strategic planning effort and put out the best possible plan their collective and collaborative talents can produce.

◆ If the organization lacks the skills, the resources, or the knowledge to aggressively and confidently develop, execute, and implement a solid Strategic Business Plan on its own and has not accessed the services of a skilled, knowledgeable, and capable outside facilitator to provide guidance.

> *"In any moment of decision, the best thing you can do is the right thing, the next best thing is the wrong thing, and the worst thing you can do is nothing."*
>
> *Theodore Roosevelt*

THE MOST POTENT REASON FOR BUSINESS PLANNING: THE BEST SURPRISE IS *NO* SURPRISE!

The number one fear or dread of every business owner or manager is an unanticipated surprise. It is an omnipresent anxiety for many. The kind of emotional jolt that forces you awake in the middle of the night. It leaves you staring for hours at the ceiling or into the black pool of the darkness above your bed, leaving you drenched in the sweat of your fears, pondering the great range of possible miseries that might descend upon you and your business at any moment. You dread getting whacked, without warning. It is the unexpected, crippling power of the unknown. It is comprised of the avalanche of unanticipated events that might rob you of your sleep, of your assets, of your success. When you least expect it and least need it.

Shocks delivered in the form of these surprises come in many forms—

◆ Dramatic shifts in the economy

◆ Labor unrest

◆ Breakdowns in the supply chain

◆ Damaging shifts in legislation

◆ Litigious actions, both frivolous and justifiable

◆ Bankruptcy of key customers or suppliers

◆ Institutions reneging on financial commitments

◆ Order cancellations by customers or clients

◆ The loss of key employees

◆ Major theft or other loss of key assets

◆ Disastrous loss of equipment or facilities

The list could go on and on, virtually without end. At the end of every surprise that comes along in the life of a business, or in the life of a business owner, there are phrases that are inevitably heard: *"If only I would have known. . . ."* *"If I only could have seen it coming. . . ."* *"I should have been on top of this sooner. . . ."* *"I could have done something about it if only. . . ."* *"I would have reacted better if I'd have had more warning. . . ."* It is an endless round of hand wringing and second guessing. The saddest thing, on reflection, for many is that it all could have been so readily and easily avoided.

> *"To be prepared is half the victory."*
>
> ### Miguel de Cervantes

How can you protect yourself from such potentially painful and debilitating surprises? The answer is to take the initiative. Actively take the steps and gather the knowledge that will allow you to better know, in advance, what might happen. Fortify yourself and your organization with freshly gathered awareness. Apply the knowledge to know in advance, and make decisions and contingency lists in confident anticipation of bad things happening to you and your business when you least need them. *Making decisions in advance*—having a series of well thought out, researched, methodically thorough and systematic decisions for the future—is what you want and need to do to avoid the pain of untimely surprises. It is formalizing and crystallizing the power of your awareness and strategic contingency thinking in the form of a plan. For your business and for your own personal peace of mind, it is an official, written Strategic Business Plan.

Great competitive advantage opportunities exist for those business owners and their leadership teams willing to step up, make the commitment, and do the work necessary to design, develop, and build a thoughtful Strategic Business Plan for their companies.

> *"Few people have any next, they live from hand to mouth without a plan, and are always at the end of their line."*
>
> ### Ralph Waldo Emerson

TYPES OF STRATEGIC BUSINESS PLANS

There are four primary types of strategic business plans, each written for differing individual applications and distinct audiences:

◆ Operational Business Plan

◆ Feasibility Business Plan

◆ Complete Business Plan

◆ Summary Business Plan

Strategic Business Planning Realities in the Competitive Marketplace

Recent studies into the day-to-day business of home builders has revealed a correlation with the benefits of business plans. For example, An Investigation of Management Practices Used in Small-Volume Home Building Companies of the United States is based on a survey of 359 home builders, who built from 1 to 25 new homes in 1999. Among the study findings are these:

On Business Planning

◆ *12.26% of the surveyed companies had written business plans*
◆ *17.55% had a written mission statement*
◆ *14.21% indicated they had written operating budgets*
◆ *More than two-thirds (69.92%) indicated they had not implemented any formal planning procedures*
◆ *Less than one-fourth (23.68%) of the companies planned cash flows more than one month in advance*
◆ *5.06% hired outside business consultants on a regular basis*
◆ *71.91% had never used an outside business consultant or advisor*

On Accounting Practices and Perceived Profitability

◆ *When comparing themselves with other homebuilding companies of similar size, 41.67% thought they were more profitable*
◆ *Almost two-thirds (60.97%) indicated the company officer responsible for accounting was proficient in analyzing and understanding financial statements*
◆ *38.31% reported that income statements were reviewed more frequently than once a quarter*
◆ *42.40% reported reviewing balance sheets more than once a quarter*

The length and depth of each of these four separate plans will vary with the complexity of your business. Keep in mind that you want to simplify the strategic planning process and make it more accessible and understandable for those who will participate in the effort. Understanding the differences among the four types of plans will help you select the one best suited to your needs.

OPERATIONAL BUSINESS PLAN

The operational business plan is used most frequently and is often destined for internal consumption, used by ownership, management, the board of directors, and outside advisors to guide the ongoing operating performance of the business. The operational business plan includes the annual departmental budgets and operating plans. As it's the document used to focus and align the efforts of all managers and leaders, it should be reviewed in detail and adjusted quarterly the first year and then annually. Writing a good operational business plan is the focal point of running and administering a healthy and well-managed organization. The operational business plan is usually 50 to 100 pages, depending on the complexity of the business, and includes all financial budgets and supporting data.

> "A good plan is like a road map: It shows the final
> destination and usually the best way to get there."
>
> H. Stanley Judd

FEASIBILITY BUSINESS PLAN

The feasibility business plan is an even more closely held internal document. Its purpose is to assess the viability of either a proposed new venture or a new product within an established operating business. This is considered a highly proprietary document and is not distributed outside those who have a vested role in its existence. The feasibility business plan is designed to be more practical than promotional in nature, exploring the full range of considerations required to render a "Go No Go" decision on any new venture, product, or service.

Although 80 percent of new ventures, products, or services fail within the first three to five years, a great deal of grief and financial loss can be saved if business owners correctly utilize and follow the feasibility business planning process prior to an ill-conceived or untimely launch. The typical length of a feasibility business plan runs from 10 to 20 pages.

> "If you keep thinking about what you want to do or what
> you hope will happen, you don't do it, and it won't happen."
>
> Joe Dimaggio

COMPLETE BUSINESS PLAN

The complete business plan is designed for external audiences and is used to persuade, educate, and inform readers. It is crafted to give a comprehensive picture of your business and is most often used to obtain funding, either in the form of debt or equity. This plan describes your business concept and strategic direction in explicit detail and is intended to provide full disclosure to all readers. In these applications, the audiences viewing the complete plan are customarily made up of bankers, prospective investors or backers, underwriters, selected creditors, outside advisors, strategic partners, and key stakeholders or shareholders. It is the most thorough of the four strategic plan formats and requires the greatest levels of collaboration and coordination by the management team. The complete business plan is about 60 to 130 pages or more, depending on the complexity of the business, and includes all financial budgets and supporting data.

SUMMARY BUSINESS PLAN

The summary business plan is a significantly shortened version of the complete business plan and is intended for either external or internal audiences. It highlights the most important information contained in the larger complete plan and is often pulled directly from the complete plan's executive summary. For external readers,

TABLE 1-1 CONTENTS OF THE FOUR TYPES OF STRATEGIC BUSINESS PLANS

Item Number	Content-Title of Section	Plan Type			
		Operational	Feasibility	Complete	Summary
1	Cover Page	X	X	X	X
2	Inside Title Page	X	X	X	X
3	Non-Disclosure Agreement	X	Optional	X	X
4	Table of Contents	X	Optional	X	Optional
5	Purpose of the Business Plan	X	X	X	X
6	Executive Summary	X	X	X	X
7	Company Direction	X		X	
8	Vision, Mission/Purpose, Values	X		X	X
9	Brand Promise	X		X	X
10	Company Overview	X		X	
11	Product & Service Strategies	X	X	X	
12	Market Analysis	X	X	X	
13	Sales & Marketing Plan	X		X	
14	Operations & IT Plans	X		X	
15	Financial Plan Overview	X	X	X	X
16	Issues, Goals, & Action Plans	X		X	
17	Staffing Plans	X		X	
	Financial Data Exhibits	Operational	Feasibility	Complete	Summary
18	Pro Forma Assumptions	X	X	X	
19	Pro Forma Income Statements	X	Optional	X	
20	Pro Forma Balance Sheets	X		X	
21	Pro Forma Cash Flow Forecast	X		X	
22	Key Ratios Forecast	X		X	
23	Critical Numbers Forecast	X		X	
24	Financial Analysis			X	
25	Investment Needs Outline			X	
26	Use of Funds Statement			X	
27	Accountant Review Sign-Off			X	
28	Back Cover Page	X	X	X	X
	Supporting Data Exhibits	Operational	Feasibility	Complete	Summary
29	Banking Relationship(s)	Optional		X	
30	Underwriting Relationship(s)			X	
31	Property & Equipment Leases	Optional		X	
32	Debt Contracts Disclosure	Optional		X	
33	Legal Structure Documentation			X	
34	Patents & Trademarks	Optional		X	
35	Liabilities Disclosure	Optional		X	
36	Pending Litigation or Claims	Optional		X	
37	Professional Services Providers	Optional		X	
38	Risk Analysis			X	
39	References & Potential Investors			X	

who often prefer this condensed version, the summary plan is all the detail they need. For internal readers, such as employees or key employment applicants, it is just enough detail for them to digest while enjoying an inside look at where the organization is headed.

The summary business plan is often tendered first to prospective external readers to determine if they have the interest or the need to take a look at the more in-depth complete business plan. The typical length of a summary business plan is from 12 to 25 pages.

SELECTING THE RIGHT PLAN

Now that you understand the four primary types of strategic business plans and their respective contents and uses, you will need to select the right type and size of plan for you and your business. Keeping in mind the four plan types, it is important to select the right plan based on the specific intended application of your plan. Here, again, are the four plans and their applications for you to select from:

You'll be able to select the right plan by using Table 1.2 and answering these questions:

What is the purpose of your plan?
Who is your intended audience?
How complex is your business?
How long should your written plan be?

Selecting the right plan will allow you to know how much work is involved and what sort of team you need to design and build the plan. After this decision has been made, you are ready to get serious about starting the strategic planning process.

"I just wake up and say, 'You're a bum. Go do something worthwhile today.'"

Garth Brooks

THE STRATEGIC PLANNING TEAM

After the type of plan has been selected, owners and top management will create the strategic planning group or team with people from throughout the organization.

The strategic planning group should meet initially for at least one day. Thereafter, they should plan to convene periodically during the first full year of implementation—monthly at first, then quarterly for the balance of the first year. Then, the group should meet annually to revisit performance from the previous year's plan and to establish the comprehensive and updated plan for the coming year.

TABLE 1-2 SELECTING THE RIGHT PLAN

Type of Plan	Purpose of Plan	Intended Audience	Length of Document
Operational	Operational decision making	Internal	50–100 pages
Feasibility	Test viability of ideas, products, or services	Internal	10–20 pages
Complete	Raise capital	External	60–130 pages
	Educate		
	Persuade		
Summary	Raise capital	Internal & external	12–25 pages
	Qualify interest		

Bear in mind that in today's business environment, many organizations find that portions of their Strategic Business Plan may not survive a full year. Indeed, in the process of building and implementing a strategic plan, you should expect your plan to undergo perpetual scrutiny, periodic review, and you and your key leaders should remain open to continuous revision.

"Unfortunately, regret is a part of human existence. To defeat it, you must confront your fears before the opportunity is lost. If you wait, the regret will eat away at you for the rest of your life."

Clint Greenleaf

ACTION INITIATORS

- ◆ Decide if you and your organization need a strategic plan.
- ◆ Determine why you need a business plan.
- ◆ If the need is valid, conclude whether RIGHT NOW is the best time to take on the task of creating a strategic plan.
- ◆ If not, determine what the potential costs may be if you delay. Are these costs you're willing to pay?
- ◆ If so, decide which of the four plan types best suits your needs.
- ◆ Lay out the initial timeframes to move forward into developing your Strategic Business Plan.

2

THE STRATEGIC GROWTH SYSTEM

*"Nobody sets out with the intention of planning to fail. No.
Those who fail, most often, are guilty of failing to properly plan."*

Benjamin Franklin

Building an effective business plan involves following seven simple steps. These steps are based on a time-tested process of strategic business planning that draws on fundamental tools and techniques, sound business practices, and specific actions that will carry you toward your vision for the future. The Seven-Step Strategic Growth System incorporates rudiments of both the Executive Mentors & Trainers programs and the Gazelles/Masters of Business Dynamics programs for mastering the management of fast-growth companies. In reality, these rudiments are applicable to any company or organization, fast-growth or not. Any organization and any company, regardless of industry, can benefit from the awareness, knowledge, and application of these systems, processes, and techniques.

GROWTH RATE

One of the initial areas you need to examine and identify is your organization's current orientation to growth. As you assess the organization today, what is your growth rate? The following chart will help you define and classify your organization.

To verify where your organization resides on this table, look back over the last three years of annual financial performance.

◆ What were the revenue and profitability trends during the past three years?

◆ Has your revenue growth rate accelerated, declined, or is it flat?

◆ Has your profitability growth accelerated, remained steady, or declined?

◆ Have margins grown, remained steady, or eroded?

Pinpointing the growth rate of your business is an essential reality check for you to confront as you look toward the future of your organization. It provides an immediate reference point for how much work is ahead in the business planning process.

Growth rate awareness is important in the business planning process for a number of other reasons. First, the trends may dictate a call to action as you embark on the strategic planning process.

◆ What does the trend in revenue and profitability growth tell you about your organization?

◆ What impact is the general economy in your market(s) having on your trends?

**TABLE 2-1 GROWTH RATES: WHERE ARE
YOU AND YOUR BUSINESS RIGHT NOW**

Growth Classification	Growth Rates
Regressive growth	Less than zero
No growth	Zero
Marginal or slow growth	0–5%
Moderate growth	6–15%
Fast growth	15%+

◆ If the current trend will likely *not* get you to where you'd like to be, as an organization, what do you need to do about it?

◆ If the present trends are unacceptable, where do you want your organization's growth rate to be in the future?

◆ What growth rate will you need to lead and manage your organization toward future success?

"You miss 100% of the shots you never take."

Wayne Gretzky

THREE BARRIERS TO GROWTH

In his book *Mastering the Rockefeller Habits,* Verne Harnish talks about what the presidents and CEOs of fast-growing companies know that you may not know about how best to build a powerful, industry-leading business. Verne states three common barriers to growth that must be met and mastered.

◆ The need for the leadership team to grow, as individual and collective leaders, in their abilities to predict, plan, and delegate

◆ The need for proven systems and structures to handle the complexity and simplify the management that comes with growth

◆ The need to navigate the increasingly tricky market dynamics that mark your arrival in a larger market-place, driven by growth and accented by the higher visibility and market presence that goes along with it

These needs are addressed in the Seven-Step Strategic Growth program detailed in this chapter and by the executive mentors & trainers and gazelles/MBD processes that comprise it.

*"Whatever failures I have known, whatever errors I have committed, whatever follies I
have witnessed in private and public life have been the consequence of action without thought."*

Bernard Baruch

SEVEN PLANNING STEPS

The seven steps of the strategic growth system spill over into one another, in a process we call cascading. The seven distinct and important steps help build in volume; add clarity; increase confidence, communication, and

TABLE 2-2 SEVEN-STEP STRATEGIC GROWTH PROGRAM

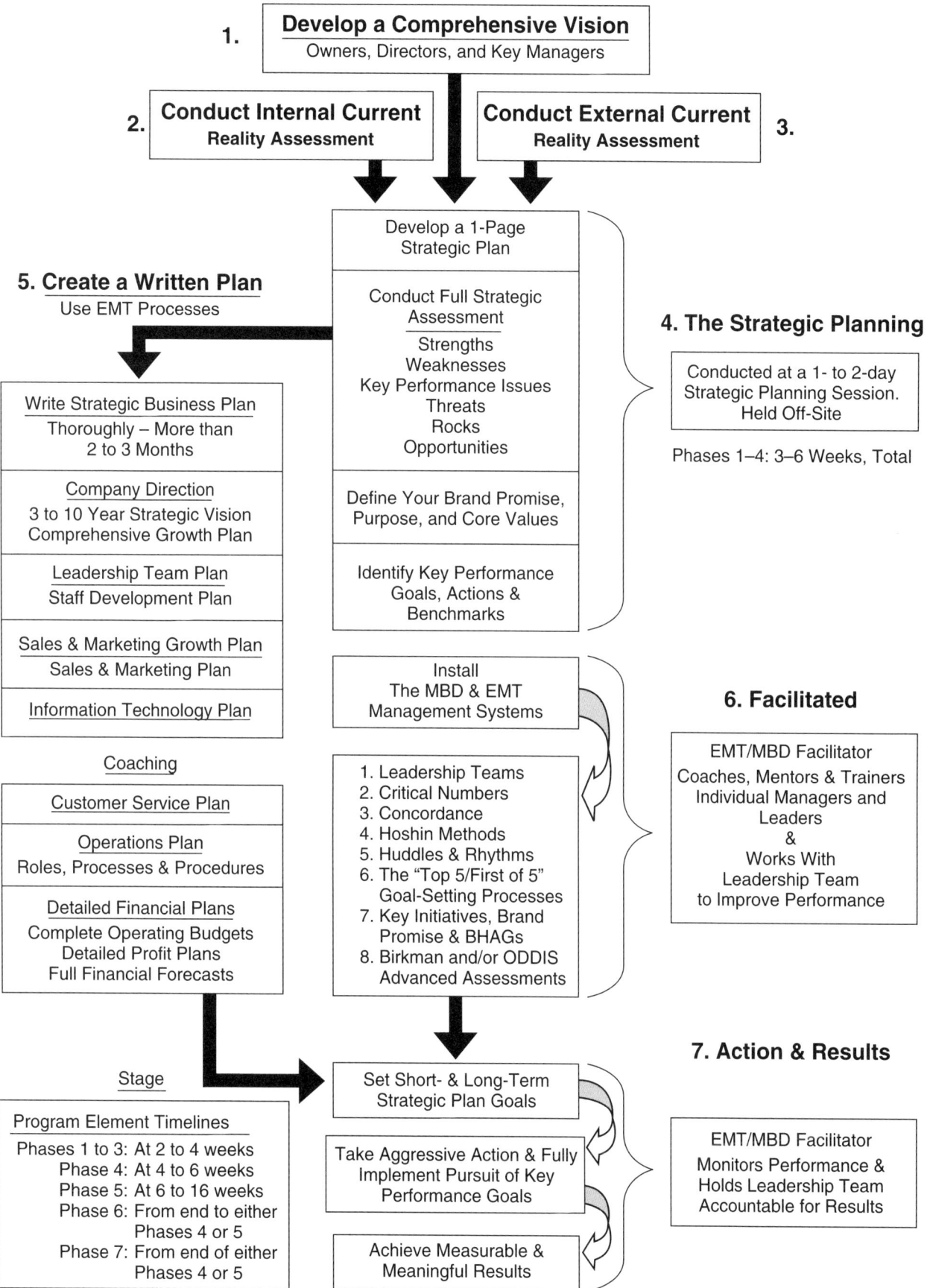

1. Develop a Comprehensive Vision
Owners, Directors, and Key Managers

2. Conduct Internal Current Reality Assessment

3. Conduct External Current Reality Assessment

Develop a 1-Page
Strategic Plan

Conduct Full Strategic
Assessment
Strengths
Weaknesses
Key Performance Issues
Threats
Rocks
Opportunities

Define Your Brand Promise,
Purpose, and Core Values

Identify Key Performance
Goals, Actions &
Benchmarks

5. Create a Written Plan
Use EMT Processes

Write Strategic Business Plan
Thoroughly – More than
2 to 3 Months

Company Direction
3 to 10 Year Strategic Vision
Comprehensive Growth Plan

Leadership Team Plan
Staff Development Plan

Sales & Marketing Growth Plan
Sales & Marketing Plan

Information Technology Plan

Coaching

Customer Service Plan

Operations Plan
Roles, Processes & Procedures

Detailed Financial Plans
Complete Operating Budgets
Detailed Profit Plans
Full Financial Forecasts

4. The Strategic Planning

Conducted at a 1- to 2-day
Strategic Planning Session.
Held Off-Site

Phases 1–4: 3–6 Weeks, Total

Install
The MBD & EMT
Management Systems

1. Leadership Teams
2. Critical Numbers
3. Concordance
4. Hoshin Methods
5. Huddles & Rhythms
6. The "Top 5/First of 5"
   Goal-Setting Processes
7. Key Initiatives, Brand
   Promise & BHAGs
8. Birkman and/or ODDIS
   Advanced Assessments

6. Facilitated

EMT/MBD Facilitator
Coaches, Mentors & Trainers
Individual Managers and
Leaders
&
Works With
Leadership Team
to Improve Performance

Stage

Program Element Timelines
Phases 1 to 3: At 2 to 4 weeks
Phase 4: At 4 to 6 weeks
Phase 5: At 6 to 16 weeks
Phase 6: From end to either
         Phases 4 or 5
Phase 7: From end of either
         Phases 4 or 5

Set Short- & Long-Term
Strategic Plan Goals

Take Aggressive Action & Fully
Implement Pursuit of Key
Performance Goals

Achieve Measurable &
Meaningful Results

7. Action & Results

EMT/MBD Facilitator
Monitors Performance &
Holds Leadership Team
Accountable for Results

momentum; and lead to personal and professional growth. The two ultimate destinations for this easy-to-follow system are—

1. Improved results
2. Stronger working relationships

Sequentially followed, the seven steps allow you to build a thorough, well-crafted plan, dealing effectively with your needs, dreams, and any stark current realities. While doing so, you are developing a cohesive way to communicate, elevate, and reinforce the details of the plan in the mind of each person having vested interests.

"At all times it is better to have a method."

Mark Caine

STEP 1. DEVELOPING A COMPREHENSIVE VISION

The first step in the strategic growth system requires you to think intensely and thoroughly about the future of your organization. Think about what you *want* and *need* the future to look like, so it can meet your needs and expectations. The vision includes input from all owners of the business and can include input from the key leaders, outside of ownership, who may play valuable roles in developing, influencing, executing, or ensuring the future performance and success of the organization.

The vision is built from a series of vital questions, posed to ownership and leadership, that probe each respondent's thoughts and feelings on the organization's future. What would the organization be like if it were perfect? Perfect in concept, perfect in design, perfect in execution, perfect in performance?

This first step takes the average owner, or group of owners and/or key leaders, from a week to six weeks to complete. The actual length of time depends on what other issues, crises, or opportunities are making time demands on those providing vision input. The average duration of this first step is between two and four weeks.

"You will become as small as your controlling desire,
as great as your dominant aspiration."

James Allen

STEPS 2 & 3. GATHERING INTERNAL AND EXTERNAL FEEDBACK

Feedback is the first reality check. It allows you to formally take the pulse of those on the frontlines of your business—your managers, your employees, your suppliers, and your customers. It allows you to get closer to the truths these people have about your business. It forces you to evaluate the strengths, weaknesses, and sentiments of the key relationships that influence present performance and preordain future success.

Internal and external feedback is gathered from customized, circulated surveys designed to provide ownership and leadership with an unadulterated look at itself, as seen through the eyes of a representative sampling of qualified and opinionated observers. Preferably collected, compiled, and administered by a neutral third party, such an outside facilitator, it is designed to confidentially protect the sources of the feedback. This encourages all respondents to tell their truths without concerns over possible retribution should their source be identified directly by the in-house owners or managers. By using an outside source to set up and compile the internal and external current reality surveys, you create your best prospect for hearing the whole truth. This leads to better decision making for you and your company.

These two steps, 2 and 3, can run concurrently with step 1, the vision step, and take an average of three to six weeks to complete from the time of initial circulation of the surveys to selected respondents to the collection and compilation of all responses for planning team review.

"Do not wait; the time will never be 'just right.' Start where you stand, and work with whatever tools you may have at your command, and better tools will be found as you go along."

Napoleon Hill

STEP 4. THE STRATEGIC PLANNING SESSION

The Strategic Planning Session is the second reality check. This session, running a day or two, is usually held off-site, away from the business and free from the distractions that can sap individual or planning team concentration. It's in this fourth step that the draft vision is shared with the entire Strategic Planning Team for the first time, reviewing it in specific detail, breaking it down and tearing it apart piece by piece, ensuring it passes full inspection. Any and all suggestions for improvement of the vision are explored and incorporated into a revised and fine-tuned final vision, which will later be presented to the entire organization.

The Strategic Planning Session is also where the entire Strategic Planning Team first reviews the internal and external survey feedback. The team goes through the feedback methodically, assessing the strengths, weaknesses, opportunities, threats, and other key issues identified as significant for the organization. Whatever the feedback, it is truly a moment of truth for the organization, and it sets the important tone for the balance of the strategic planning process. The content of the feedback outlines and highlights the magnitude of decisions required to move the organization forward and deal effectively with the realities facing it.

The Strategic Planning Session is also the forum wherein the organization defines its purpose, brand promise, core values, key performance issues and goals, critical numbers, performance benchmarks, and immediate actions to impact and improve performance. In addressing these important details, the organization makes a commitment to urgently tackle those areas that are affecting results. It also provides clarity about what *is* and *is not* important.

When the session concludes, responsibilities and accountabilities have been assumed by or assigned to the most appropriate individuals for researching and writing the plan. Very little in the way of confusion will be left to anyone's imagination.

STEP 5. CREATE A WRITTEN STRATEGIC BUSINESS PLAN

This fifth step represents the greatest challenge and the greatest opportunity for you and your Strategic Planning Team. As the tasks involved in writing the Strategic Business Plan must be done within and around everyone's existing job responsibilities and workloads, this step of the process can take two to four months to complete. The ability of all designated plan writers to free themselves from existing time commitments and aggressively redirect their time toward writing their assigned portions of the plan determines how swiftly this step can be concluded. An important consideration to keep in mind, for all plan writing participants, is to be *more thorough than swift* in this responsibility.

Creating a useful written Strategic Business Plan is a methodical process of directed research, guided discovery, and difficult questions that must be faced and factored into the plan.. In today's business environment, the plan can cover a period as short as 1 to 3 years or 10 or more years away. Reality and expediency dictate that elevated thought and attention go into accurately and dependably developing the short- to intermediate-term plan. Long-term considerations, strategies, and actions need to be reviewed and updated periodically as new economic and market realities emerge and crystallize over time. An important element to remember, even as you and your team begin the process of writing, is that your plan needs to remain flexible and readily adaptive to changing levels of self-awareness and fluctuating market conditions.

The specific areas the written plan address are—

◆ Company direction

◆ Product and service strategies

◆ Market analyses

◆ Sales and marketing strategies and action plans

◆ Operations strategies and action plans

◆ Information technology plans

◆ Customer service strategies and action plans

◆ Detailed financial information and strategies

◆ Staffing plans and budgets

The entire plan writing step is guided by specific questions that prompt the writers of each plan section to think carefully and completely about their conclusions. The questions lead the writers to develop the What to Do, the Why, the Who, and By When of each determined action. The methods employed in this step are designed to confidently direct the plan writers to complete the plan in a timely, thorough, and beneficial manner, aligned to the applications of the plan as defined and selected from Table 1.1 in Chapter 1.

> *"There is no substitute for accurate knowledge. Know yourself,
> know your business, and know your men."*
>
> *Randall Jacobs*

STEP 6. INVEST IN FUTURE LEADERS

Commencing at the end of steps 4 or 5, step 6 is an essential part of preparing yourself and your key leaders to grow in skill levels and confidence. As you formalize your vision, put in motion the decisions made at the Strategic Planning Session, and begin the disciplined process of writing your plan, ask yourself three important questions:

◆ Am I ready for this?

◆ Is my company ready for this?

◆ Are my key people ready for this?
Ready for what, you ask? Capable and confident enough to drive the planning processes and pursue full and successful execution of the decisions you're making to grow your company.

◆ Do you have the knowledge, skill, expertise, and commitment levels to drive yourself and your team toward your vision, while optimizing performance and minimizing stresses along the way?

◆ Who are the stronger, more dependable players on your team?

◆ Where are the weaker links in your organization?

◆ How are you preparing them to prepare themselves to be better leaders and more effective managers?

◆ Are the systems and processes you're presently using to operate and administer your organization producing the kinds of results that meet your needs?

◆ If not, what's working in your favor, and what's working against your interests?

◆ How are you and the other members of your team executing on the fundamentals of leadership and management within your organization?

Step 6 will prepare you and your key leaders to be better, more effective, more confident, and produce better results as you begin to implement and work your plan. It's about acquiring the knowledge and skills, the habits and patterns of behavior that lead to success and higher levels of satisfaction from your efforts. This step is an investment in your own professional and personal development, becoming a more valuable resource for your organization.

> *"There are risks and costs to a program of action, but they are far less than the long-range risks and costs of comfortable inaction."*
>
> *John F. Kennedy*

STEP 7. TAKE ACTION AND DELIVER RESULTS

Step 7 allows for you to regularly monitor performance of your plan goals and to hold the individual and collective members of the leadership team accountable for their commitments for results.

As with step 6, step 7 also commences at the end of either step 4 or 5 and then becomes a perpetual part of your organizational processes. Step 7 becomes an essential discipline that is integrated into your organization's culture. Often aided by the services of an outside facilitator, this step forces the team to pay close attention to implementing the plan in an aggressive and timely manner, achieving the milestones that differentiate success from failure. Taking action and delivering results defines your organization and distinguishes it from other companies.

ACTION INITIATORS

- ◆ Identify your historical growth rate and growth trends.
- ◆ Determine if the growth trend is acceptable to you.
- ◆ Establish the desired *future* growth rate for your organization.
- ◆ Familiarize yourself with the 7-Step Strategic Growth Program.
- ◆ Determine where you and your organization are in the seven steps in terms of readiness and need.
- ◆ Decide which of the seven steps will mark your organization's starting point.
- ◆ Initiate the decision to proceed into the strategic growth program.
- ◆ Announce your decision to your core team of leaders and to your organization.
- ◆ Enlist the support of everyone in your organization to begin and complete the strategic growth program in a thorough and timely manner.

3

THE VISION

"We should not let our fears hold us back from pursuing our hopes."

John F. Kennedy

The company's vision reflects the desires and aspirations of the owners and key leaders. It's the ideal and ultimate destination where the business or organization is headed as it looks to the future, under the skillful guidance of ownership, top management, and key employees. It is a clear, written reflection of where the business or organization wants to be (or needs to be) at a point in the future, to both capitalize on potential and fulfill the personal and professional goals of ownership, management, and employees.

The organization's owners need to develop and embrace a common vision that will allow them to meet their individual goals, allowing each to get what they want out of the organization, given successful financial performance of the organization.

"It's tough to make predictions, especially about the future."

Yogi Berra

EVALUATE THE COMPANY'S VISION

If there are several owners, each one should independently draft his or her own vision for the organization, subsequently meeting to share personal visions. Although it is unnecessary to combine the visions into a single document at this early point, care should be taken to note both shared and conflicting visions between owners and leaders. If conflicts are apparent, it often is helpful to have a neutral facilitator help steer a group of owners and leaders through this important step of discovery and self-awareness.

The owner's vision will describe such things as:

◆ Organization's forecast of annual revenues

◆ Desired levels of profitability

◆ Growth rates

◆ Acceptable levels of indebtedness

◆ Product and service offerings

◆ Current and future customer profiles

◆ Anticipated expansion of markets

◆ Expansion of locations

◆ Accomplishments and aspirations for the organization

◆ Contributions to society

◆ Technologies to increase productivity and performance

◆ Future potential leadership and ownership

◆ Philosophies, values, self-concept, and public image

◆ Organizational opportunities

◆ Desired employee attributes

◆ Survival and market share strategies

◆ Specific roles, degrees of commitment, personal income levels, and other aspiration levels of the owners and the organization's key people

Drafting the owner's vision is a fundamental first step in the strategic planning process. It describes how those at the helm desire the organization to be as it matures. Those involved in this drafting process should try to include at least five significant goals they want to see accomplished during the organization's life span. This will give added dimension to the imagery created by the contributors in the vision process.

The outcome that all parties seek in the owner's vision drafting process is to imagine the organization as it will be in the future. To do this, begin with the end in mind. This will allow you to move toward your desired destination.

*"What every man needs, regardless of his job or the kind of work he is doing,
is a vision of what his place is and may be. He needs an objective and a purpose.
He needs a feeling and a belief that he has some worthwhile thing to do.*

*What this is no one can tell him. It must be his own creation. Its success will
be measured by the nature of his vision, what he has done to equip himself,
and how well he has performed along the line of its development."*

Joseph M. Dodge

DEFINE THE OWNER'S VISION

A clearly defined and well-written owner's vision conveys value and benefits in several significant ways. First, a vision statement defines your organization's direction, character, and personality. It allows anyone interested in your organization to visualize and respond to it. It helps people see your organization as you and your key people view it, both now and into the future, and not simply as an impersonal and lifeless statement on a piece of paper. It brings your organization's appealing qualities, and future promise, into a more tangible clarity.

Second, putting personality into your plan and vision will make for more interesting reading. This can make the difference in your vision and plan actually being read and reviewed by an interested investor, buyer, influential third party, current employee, or prospective employee . . . or not getting read at all.

The owner's vision should outline a path for your organization to stretch both its potential and its possibilities. Yet it must still remain simple, believable, and achievable in the minds of employees and managers and be easily understood and communicated by everyone in the organization. All people involved and associated with your organization should be able to comprehend and relate to the vision. In the real world, the wisest vision provides believable yet inspiring aspirations and real products and services that real people will buy . . . and for which you will get paid!

> *"I have always wanted to be somebody, but I see now I should have been more specific."*
>
> *Lily Tomlin*

DEFINE THE VISION

The process of physically writing and refining the vision forces the owner(s) and/or leaders to think about what the ultimate goals and destinations are, for both the organization and for themselves. It forces contributors to expand their perspectives, to examine their innermost thoughts, feelings, fears, and expectations; to clarify the purpose for which their organization exists; and to clearly identify what is really important for them.

As each owner independently discovers a vision, each is forced to clarify and express deepest values and aspirations in specific terms. This process imprints and crystallizes an owner's or leader's true values that will be defined in the vision and the strategic plan.

> *"Lord, grant that I may always desire more than I can accomplish."*
>
> *Michelangelo*

DIFFERENT VISIONS ADDRESS DIFFERENT NEEDS

As you begin developing your vision, you may want to consider creating several different versions of your vision, to serve or address a variety of differing needs. Determine this by answering the question, "How will you use your vision and plan?"

◆ To attract partners, investors, and/or capital?

◆ To inspire and direct your staff?

◆ To aid in the development and production of your strategic plan?

◆ To make strategic and tactical decisions?

◆ To attract and retain top talent?

◆ To energize and configure your organization to deliver a breakthrough in performance?

All of the applications are valid, so you may find it beneficial to have several versions of your vision, crafted to appeal to different audiences. There will likely be sensitive or proprietary information in your vision you may wish to circulate and communicate internally that would not be prudent to circulate externally. Such carefully guarded information may include projections for revenues, profitability, debt levels, expansion plans, and new products.

> *"Some self-confronting questions: Where do I want to be at any given time?*
> *How am I going to get there? What do I have to do to get myself from where I am*
> *to where I want to be? and What's the first small step I can take to get moving?"*
>
> *George A. Ford*

IDENTIFY YOUR SPECIFIC NEEDS

As you prepare to write the vision, it is important that you place your attention and efforts squarely on the specific destinations you seek. It is a time for you to be a bit selfish and to ask the question, "What's in it for me?"

◆ Why are you doing this strategic planning process?

◆ Is it safe to say that if your business were producing results that satisfied you 100 percent at this time, you'd likely be doing something entirely different than reading this book?

◆ What needs are not being addressed satisfactorily at this time?

◆ What areas of your life, either personally or professionally, are in need of attention?

◆ What areas of your life are not producing the results you were hoping for?

As you'll see from the vision statement questions that follow in this chapter, you will examine more than simply what you want for your organization's future. It is important to examine your own motivators, satisfiers, and payoffs in driving and directing the efforts of your organization to achieve a worthy vision and future.

At this point, do you know how the successful achievement of your organization's vision will help you achieve personal life balance and quality of life that is your due? If not, the list of vision-building questions in this chapter will assist you in coming to terms with your own best interests, and expose your feelings in the process.

"The best way to predict the future is to invent it."

Alan Kay

Focus on the Ends Rather Than on the Means

There is a very natural danger we must point out as you begin to look to your destination. In basic human psychology, the average person finds it difficult to look to their desired future without consciously or unconsciously considering the obstacles and limitations. Do not fall into the trap of reducing or restricting your aspirations and desires through limits imposed on your thinking by either previous experience or the current realities of scarce resources.

Keep in mind that you are looking to create a strong, appealing, compelling vision of what you want your ideal destination to be as you plan for the future. To optimize the power of your imagination and the creative function in developing your vision, you need to improve the quality of your thinking. To do this, you must think only about the ideal destination for you and your organization. You must work to describe the ideal destination in terms that are free of limitation, free of restriction.

Focus On the What Rather Than on the How

Another natural danger that paralyzes many who begin the vision-building process is the tendency to begin pondering *how* to achieve the *what*. Once again, this natural phenomenon works against you as you begin to craft your vision.

Release your full imagination on the vision-building process, without worrying about the *how* of achieving the vision that emerges. The *how* will come later, and will take care of itself in the strategic planning process.

You do not need to know any of the *how's* at this point. You do not need to be certain, right now, as to how you are going to get to any of the destinations you define in your vision. You do need to develop an effective way to communicate your destination to those in your organization that either have a vested interest in the outcome or can play a role in helping you achieve your vision.

WRITE THE VISION

Writing vision narratives is as much a process of discovery as it is a process of creation. This is a process that may require some patience. Do not feel you have to rush through this process. Don't set rigid timetables for completion. The goal is to get it right for yourself and your organization. The process is designed to ensure that you ask yourself the right questions and that you think deeply about your own values and aspirations. Be sure to include—

♦ What you want to do

♦ What you want to accomplish

♦ What contributions you want to make

♦ What you want to be

♦ What character strengths you want to possess and display

♦ What qualities, skills, and values you want to cultivate, embody, and grow

DEFINE THE IDEAL DESTINATION

♦ What's the ideal destination for both you and your organization 1, 3, 5, and 10 years from now?

♦ When all is said and done, what do the leaders want to achieve?

♦ What will be the owner's legacy?

♦ What do the leaders want to be?

♦ What do the leaders want to have?

♦ What do the leaders want to do?

♦ When they retire or sell how do the owners and stakeholders want themselves and the organization described and remembered?

WRITE THE OWNER'S VISION STATEMENT

When you begin writing your vision for the organization, direct your efforts toward answering, in precise and exacting detail, the questions that will define in graphic terms what you want the organization to be in 3 to 10 or more years. Among the important questions you will want to ask yourself and answer honestly are the following:

♦ How will the organization be recognized within your industry?

♦ What noteworthy accomplishments will the organization achieve?

♦ What will your organization's public image and standing in the community look like?

- What will be your organization's primary products and services?

- In which markets will your organization compete?

- In which locations will you maintain offices?

- Who will be your valued and optimal customers?

- How will your customers view your organization?

- What revenue and profit levels will your organization be driving and enjoying?

- What rate of growth will your organization be experiencing?

- What will your organization's commitments be toward achieving financial objectives?

- What will shareholder equity look like?

- What will your debt structure look like?

- Who will be your organization's key leaders?

- What benefits will key managers and leaders be receiving from the organization?

- What benefits will employees be receiving from the organization?

- What attitudes will your organization have about its employees?

- What kinds of technology will you be using?

- What will your organization's unique strengths include?

- What important values will your organization embody?

- What basic beliefs, attitudes, aspirations, and philosophical priorities are evident?

- What will your organization be contributing to society?

On a more personally professional note, ask yourself—

- What will your optimal role and duties within the organization look like to you?

- What will your own desired compensation levels look like?

- What benefits will you be receiving from your organization?

- When do you want to exit your role and responsibilities in the organization?

- What will your own exit strategy look like, if it were optimal?

- Who will succeed you as owner(s) of the organization?

And on an even more personal note, ask yourself—

◆ What level of security do you seek for the future?

◆ Creating more personal time for yourself would provide what benefits and outcomes?

◆ Creating more time to spend with your family would provide what benefits and outcomes?

◆ What would you do with greater time for personal growth and development?

◆ What would you do with more time for professional growth and improvement?

◆ What would a perfectly balanced life look like for you, from this point forward?

◆ What would a perfectly fulfilling life look like for you, from this point forward?

Coming to very thorough, personal terms with each of these questions is what you need to do before you can move effectively forward in the process. You need to address these questions in a systematic way in the vision for yourself and your organization.

CREATE THE MISSION AND PURPOSE

A mission statement, or purpose statement as it is often called, reflects a vision and describes the purpose for which an organization exists. It describes *why* we do what we choose to do. It is crafted to be both a practical and a philosophical statement. It is used as a declaration of our deep and profound commitment to our cause and purpose or mission.

If the organization or individual fulfills its well-defined purpose or mission, it likely will move aggressively toward its vision. If it does not fulfill its mission, it will likely fall short of its vision.

The mission statement is created as part of the vision process, at this initial point in the planning cycle, or during the Strategic Planning Session itself, as detailed in Chapter 6. Regardless of when it is developed, the mission statement should reflect the vision of the owners and the leaders. It ought to be crafted to integrate the attitudes and desires of the entire management team. It must take into account the perceptions, the needs, and the expectations of individuals, departments, and the overall organization. The mission statement should be summed up in a few short sentences or, at most, a few short paragraphs.

The mission statement will embody the elements of personal and organizational leadership that provide overall direction, guidance, moral grounding, meaning, and purpose to the efforts of all individuals participating in the creation of the vision, mission, and values for your organization. *Everything* the organization does in the future should be consistent and in compliance with the content and intent of the mission, purpose, and values statements.

> *"The only limits, as always, are those of vision."*
>
> *James Broughton*

TURN VISIONS INTO ORGANIZATIONAL GOALS

Have you ever noticed the great lengths to which people will go to avoid doing precisely what needs to be done? Avoiding the essential, hard, often heavy-lifting dirty work marks the difference between progress and procrastination. For example: There's no better time to begin cleaning or organizing the desk or workstation than just before an important project or deadline is due. In cognitive psychology, they have a term for it: creative avoidance. It's not that you don't necessarily know what to do. It's that *we don't want to do it,* even though we may, or may not, consciously know better.

The best way to limit creative avoidance is to keep it simple, and manageable, through building goals to support your vision and strategic plan. Top 5 and first of 5 goal setting utilizes this approach with fast-growth clients.

THE TOP 5 AND FIRST OF 5 GOALS

The organization with too many priorities has no real priorities at all.

To align and focus yourself and your staff around accomplishing the goals and tasks that will *truly* make a difference in your organization's performance, keep it simple: Clearly articulate the five most important priorities that **must** be addressed or achieved to move the team or organization, or yourself, to the next level of performance *at any given time.*

Determine Top 5 and First of 5

◆ Ask yourself, "What do I need to be doing today (or this month, quarter, or year) to keep this company moving toward its goals, at the speed the market demands of us?"

◆ Make a list of the five urgent tasks or goals that answer the question, above, for periods covering the next 30 days, 90 days, 180 days, 270 days, and year.

◆ To determine your own first of 5, ask yourself, "From the list of 5 goals I've identified, *what single item hurts the most,* right now."

To drive the process into your team or organization—

◆ Have each member of your team or organization adopt this same process, setting individual and/or departmental top 5 and first of 5 goals.

◆ Have each team member set top 5 and first of 5 goals for each month, each quarter, and each fiscal year.

◆ On a monthly, quarterly, and an annual basis, review each team member's performance in achieving or exceeding their top 5 and first of 5 goals. Celebrate successes and learn from any shortfalls. Insist on immediate corrective action for shortfalls.

Set Top 5 and First of 5 Goals That Align With Your Vision

After you've created the initial top 5 and first of 5 goals, test the validity of the goals with an elementary question:

"Will this goal get me closer to my vision, or will it take me further away from achieving my vision?"

The acid test of decision making is also very simple:

◆ If the goal will take you closer to your vision, you pursue it.

◆ If the goal takes you further away from achieving your vision, you drop it. Fast. Without second guessing. Without regret.

With the above in mind, turn your attention to your next task: creating the top 5 and first of 5 goals to support your own vision.

> *"Set your expectations high; find men and women whose integrity and values you respect; get their agreement on a course of action; and give them your ultimate trust."*
>
> *John Akers*

SHARE THE VISION

Share the vision with fellow owners, partners, and key leaders. You may find that even among the closest of owners, partners, or key people, there will be some surprises and differences that surface as you compare or share your individualized visions. The process of facilitated sharing is an enlightening process and well worth all the careful reflective time and thought you put into preparing and sharing your individual owner's vision.

Initial owners' visions need not be in strict agreement. What is important is that the visions of owners, partners, and key leaders be compatible, not in significant conflict or opposition. If conflict does emerge you may want to bring in a facilitator to conduct a professionally negotiated resolution of differences before moving on to the next phase of the strategic planning process. This process allows negotiation to take place between owners and leaders, creating an owner's vision that all can endorse.

The refinement of the owner's vision precedes and influences the writing of the organization's mission statement. The leaders present their refined vision at the start of the strategic planning meeting, as covered in Chapter 6. With the draft of the owner's vision in mind, the participants in the strategic planning meeting can then finalize the vision and write a solid, final draft of the organization's mission/purpose and values statements.

ACTION INITIATORS

- ◆ Understand the value and benefits of developing a vision for your organization.
- ◆ Define, in writing, the ideal destination for your organization, over the periods covering 1 year, 3 years, 5 years, and 10-plus years from now.
- ◆ Describe, in writing, your answers to the owner's vision questions contained in this chapter. Take three to four passes over each question, amplifying the level of detail and magnifying the level of clarity with each successive pass.
- ◆ Create a cohesive narrative version of your vision, with the intent of sharing it with other core leaders in the organization.
- ◆ Draft a mission and purpose statement for your organization.
- ◆ Understand the top 5 and first of 5 goal-setting process.
- ◆ Draft your top 5 and first of 5 goals for yourself and your organization, for periods covering the next 90 days, next 6 months, next 12 months, and the next 24 to 36 months.
- ◆ Share your draft vision, mission and purpose, and top 5 and first of 5 goals with your core leaders for initial input.

4

THE CURRENT REALITY

"Most ailing organizations have developed a functional blindness to their own defects. They are not suffering because they cannot resolve their problems but because they cannot see their problems."

John Gardner

A Current Reality Assessment serves as a baseline for business performance and as a practical tool to help everyone involved understand the depth of effort and level of urgency required.

"Unless you try something beyond what you have mastered, you will never grow."

C. R. Lawton

The Current Reality Assessment gives you the opportunity, in an organized and directed process, to ask yourself vital questions required to establish your business baseline.

◆ Where are your strengths?

◆ Where are your weaknesses?

◆ What's causing stress?

◆ What issues are causing grief?

◆ What's getting in the way?

◆ What are the elements in your working environment that are operating in your favor?

◆ What are the elements in your working environment and your methods of doing business that are working against your interests?

◆ What specific areas need to be addressed to make your organization stronger, more competitive, and resilient?

These are just some of the questions the Current Reality Assessment forces you to confront as you begin building your plan.

"Close scrutiny will show that most 'crisis situations' are opportunities to either advance or stay where you are."

Maxwell Maltz

ASSESS YOUR CURRENT REALITIES

There are no "right" or "wrong" answers in the Current Reality Assessment. And there is absolutely no value in deceiving yourself by sanitizing your answers. Neither are there bonus points for sugar-coating your responses. The only ones to feel the pain of an inaccurate assessment are you, your business, and the people who work for you.

"Honesty is the first chapter in the book of wisdom."

Thomas Jefferson

ASSESS YOUR COMPANY'S CURRENT STATE OF READINESS

Assessing your company's current state involves exposing yourself to a range of questions that you should ask yourself, on a regular basis, to better measure and assess whether you are prepared to handle the spectrum of challenges looming in front of you.

The first area to evaluate includes people, structures, and processes. The following 33 questions, which are called the EMT 33, drive to the heart of better knowing yourself and your business today. Each of the 33 questions can and should be answered with a simple "yes" or "no." If the answer is not clearly and plainly a "yes," then consider it a "no." There is no downside or penalty in being brutally honest with yourself in answering each question. There is only value to you in being absolutely honest in your appraisal.

1. Are all of your organizational goals being met?
2. Are your *most important* organizational goals being met?
3. If you were asked to write down the five *most important* organizational goals for your organization, then asked your key people to do the same, would the answers agree?
4. Do the individuals on your management team *set* measurable and specific business goals?
5. Do the individuals on your management team *achieve* their measurable business goals?
6. Are all of the key people in your organization keepers for the long term?
7. Are your key people an inseparable part of the future plans for your organization?
8. Do all of your organization's key people deliver on their commitments?
9. Do you formally and regularly assess the performance of your key people?
10. Do you provide your key people with open, honest, direct, and frank feedback? If so, do you do this on a regular and formal basis? Do you share it one-on-one?
11. Are your key people delivering results that meet your expectations?
12. Have you fully defined your leadership team so that the right people are in the right positions?
13. Are you fully capitalizing on the respective strengths of each member of your leadership team?
14. Do you have a clearly defined, understood, and respected chain of command with obvious and delineated assigned areas of accountability and responsibility?
15. Does each position in your firm have a detailed position description, defining roles, responsibilities, and latitudes of authority and decision making?
16. Do you hold regular management team meetings? If so, are they effective in helping you achieve your organizational goals?
17. Do you have a written long-term Strategic Business Plan for your organization? If so, is it current? Is it delivering acceptable results?
18. Do you have a written, detailed annual financial operating plan for your organization? If so, is current performance measuring up to plan forecasts?

19. Do you have vision, mission/purpose, and values statements for your firm? If so, are you living up to them at present?

20. Do you have a comprehensive sales and/or marketing plan for your organization? If so, is it delivering results that meet your expectations?

21. Do you have a formal sales training program or process in place? If so, is it delivering results that track with your present plan and expectations?

22. Do you have a formal and effective sales management process in place?

23. Do you have a comprehensive employee policies and procedures manual for your organization? If so, is it in full compliance with current legislation?

24. Do you have a formal and effective management and leadership skills development process for growing existing and emerging leaders? If so, is it delivering results that meet your needs and expectations?

25. Do you provide a working environment and culture in which people are encouraged to grow and develop on both professional and personal levels?

26. Are you attracting and retaining key people whose performances measure up to your needs, standards, and expectations?

27. Is employee turnover within acceptable limits?

28. Do you track, measure, monitor, and communicate productivity performance? If so, are current levels of productivity acceptable?

29. Do you have a customer service improvement program? If so, are results acceptable? Are rates of customer/client turnover within acceptable limits?

30. Does your organization have adequate funding to meet its needs?

31. Is your organization as profitable as it needs to be or as profitable as you would like it to be?

32. Are either you or your key people "leaving money on the table" in any current sales, operating, or production activities, or through "lost" opportunities?

33. If all of your business creditors asked for their receivables from your organization today, in full, could you satisfy the demand without putting your business in jeopardy?

Keep in mind that your informal self-appraisal is made up of only your immediate and personal perceptions. Do the other people on your core team hold similar perceptions? Do the people throughout your organization hold similar perceptions or do they see things differently? To learn the answers, you might have each of them independently answer this same list of questions. Then compare notes.

The purpose of the EMT 33 questions is to take an unflinching look at the realities of your business relative to organizations that are considered to be disciplined, organized, deliberate, well-managed, and self-directed. Organizations that have more of these systems and processes in place usually have a greater probability of successful performance and of surviving market downturns.

"In times like these, it is helpful to remember there have always been times like these."

Paul Harvey

ASSESS YOUR KEY PERFORMANCE ISSUES

The next area of assessment involves key performance issues facing you and your company. Key performance issues are defined as *issues that, if properly addressed, are crucial to optimizing your individual or collective organizational performance and ensure the health and longevity of your organization.*

If the leading key performance issues do not receive your immediate and urgent attention, consequences can be severe. So as you dive into assessing the key performance issues facing you and your organization, pay close attention to what emerges in your appraisal and evaluate the cost of *not* dealing with issues urgently and aggressively.

The second round of questions in the Current Reality Assessment examine key performance issues hovering over you and your company. Identify as many of these key performance issues as you can and note if they are affecting your business adversely.

FINANCIAL PERFORMANCE

◆ Increasing profits

◆ Improving cash flow

◆ Improving collections and accounts receivables

◆ Developing more working capital

◆ Getting people to be more cost-conscious

◆ Improving the quality of financial reporting

STRATEGIC POSITIONING

◆ Coping with industry consolidation

◆ Responding to price competition

◆ Dealing with rapid changes within your industry or organization

◆ Achieving sustained and controlled growth

◆ Preparing the organization for transition or succession in leadership

◆ Improving the effectiveness of business planning

◆ Putting together a business plan for the organization

LEADERSHIP

◆ Increasing the commitment levels of key people

◆ Developing the management skill levels and competencies of key people

◆ Developing more effective leadership skills among staff leaders

◆ Developing a solid work ethic in employees

◆ Motivating people within the organization

◆ Improving communication within the organization

◆ Generating more teamwork

◆ Managing a diverse workforce

- Improving working relationships inside the organization

- Developing higher levels of trust within the organization

- Creating a less-stressful working environment

- Running more effective and productive meetings

- Fostering responsibility and accountability within the organization

- Lightening the management burden for owners and top managers

SALES AND MARKETING

- Increasing revenues

- Improving sales performance

- Improving marketing performance

- Putting together a sales and marketing plan for the organization

- Improving levels of customer satisfaction

- Improving the quality of life for you, as an owner or leader

PRODUCTIVITY

- Increasing production and/or productivity

- Managing time more effectively

- Finding time to do the more important things

- Increasing the quality of your product and services output

- Using technology more effectively throughout your organization

STAFFING

- Finding and keeping good people

- Reducing turnover and associated costs

After going through the list and checking off all the pertinent issues, go back and select the five issues that represent the most urgent, troublesome, or expensive issues affecting the performance of your organization. Number them, *in descending order of impact, from 1 to 5.* These are your top 5 issues today. Your first of 5 issue is the item you selected as #1. You will finalize the top 5 and first of 5 goals for your organization in Chapter 6. Concentrate your efforts on these items as you build your goals.

Prioritizing your issues is crucial at the outset of the strategic planning effort. Another benefit from having identified and prioritized key performance issues is the complete inventory of issues you have now explored and catalogued.

◆ What are the conclusions you're drawing from this compilation?

◆ Are you feeling more positive or less positive about the magnitude of the challenges you face?

◆ Does it seem your level of control and influence over these topics is greater or lesser than you imagined and felt earlier?

◆ What level of confidence do you now have over your ability to direct the efforts of your team on these issues toward positive outcomes?

In terms of your own self-efficacy—your self-image of whether or not you can master challenges and overcome obstacles—are the issues bigger than you? Or are you bigger than the issues? Your reaction will determine whether you see these issues as obstacles or as opportunities.

> *"Nothing is predestined: The obstacles of your past can become the gateways that lead to new beginnings."*
>
> *Ralph Blum*

ASSESS YOUR WORKING ENVIRONMENT

Your current working environment is the third assessment area. This area involves evaluating the culture and atmosphere in your business.

◆ What kind of culture and atmosphere have you cultivated for your business?

◆ Are the people who work for the organization satisfied with the surroundings you've produced? Is there room for improvement?

◆ Have you built a healthy, cohesive, and harmonious workplace?

◆ Do current employees feel positive about the environment in which they work? Are they inclined to remain with the organization, despite efforts by competitors to lure them away?

◆ Are outside candidates attracted to your organization because it offers an appealing and exceptional career opportunity?

This third round of the Current Reality Assessment will help shed some valuable light on all of these questions and provide you with some definitive answers.

> *"In the middle of difficulty lies opportunity."*
>
> *Albert Einstein*

The following twelve areas contain fundamental characteristics that shed light on the quality of your business' working environment. Select on the 10-point scale where you see and appraise your organization at this moment.

1. Clarity of communication
   A. Low level of clarity (1–3)
   B. Moderate level of clarity (4–6)
   C. High level of clarity (7–10)

2. Level of honesty
   A. Low level of honesty (1–3)
   B. Moderate level of honesty (4–6)
   C. High level of honesty (7–10)

3. Level of integrity
   A. Low level of integrity (1–3)
   B. Moderate level of integrity (4–6)
   C. High level of integrity (7–10)

4. Employee satisfaction with the organization
   A. Low level of satisfaction (1–3)
   B. Moderate level of satisfaction (4–6)
   C. High level of satisfaction (7–10)

5. Employee sense of job security
   A. Low level of job security (1–3)
   B. Moderate level of job security (4–6)
   C. High level of job security (7–10)

6. Level of mutual respect
   A. Low level of respect (1–3)
   B. Moderate level of respect (4–6)
   C. High level of respect (7–10)

7. Productivity inside the organization
   A. Low level of productivity (1–3)
   B. Moderate level of productivity (4–6)
   C. High level of productivity (7–10)

8. Quality of interpersonal relationships
   A. Low level of quality (1–3)
   B. Moderate level of quality (4–6)
   C. High level of quality (7–10)

9. Inclusion of employees in the decision-making process
   A. Low level of inclusion (1–3)
   B. Moderate level of inclusion (4–6)
   C. High level of inclusion (7–10)

10. Employee enthusiasm for the organization
    A. Low level of enthusiasm (1–3)
    B. Moderate level of enthusiasm (4–6)
    C. High level of enthusiasm (7–10)

11. Level of openness within the organization
    A. Low level of openness (1–3)
    B. Moderate level of openness (4–6)
    C. High level of openness (7–10)

12. Level of blaming and shaming within the organization
    A. High level of blaming/shaming (1–3)
    B. Moderate level of blaming/shaming (4–6)
    C. Low level of blaming/shaming (7–10)

Your answers and scores tell you a lot about the quality of your organization's working environment.

◆ Have you built a close-knit, openly communicative, healthy, high-integrity organization? Or are there areas where you are vulnerable, by being considered a less desirable environment in which to work and earn a living?

◆ How do you think, or feel, your organization stacks up against your closest competitors in these twelve areas?

◆ Are you competitive?

◆ Are you superior to your competition in any of the twelve areas?

◆ Arc you noticeably inferior in any of the twelve areas?

◆ If you find yourself seriously lagging behind your perceived competitors in any of these areas, what's the cost, to you, of your shortcomings in the marketplace?

◆ What kinds of penalties might you face and what costs might you have to pay, either in the competition for great people or to secure your fair share of the market(s) in which you conduct your business?

These are all important questions for you to consider before moving forward.

"Life is tough, but it's tougher if you're stupid."

John Wayne

HOW HEALTHY AND SMART IS YOUR ORGANIZATION?

Our Gazelles colleague, Patrick Lencioni, points out that all successful organizations, regardless of what industry they operate within, share two qualities: they are smart and they are healthy.

◆ SMART equals: intelligent sales and operational strategies; solid marketing plans; products and services with valued features; and financial models that lead to competitive advantages over rivals.

◆ HEALTHY equals: eliminating politics, unhealthy relationships, confusion, chaos, and under-performers. This leads to the creation of healthier, more open relationships, which in turn produce higher trust and respect, higher morale, lower turnover, and higher overall productivity and help you develop and retain great and gifted people. It also produces a market reputation that attracts top talent to your organization.

Although both smart and healthy are required to make a *good* organization a *great* organization, most leaders focus more efforts on getting an organization smarter rather than healthier. With that in mind,

◆ Where is the balance in your organization right now?

◆ Does the balance you've created tilt toward smarter or healthier?

◆ If there's an imbalance in your working environment and in the culture of your organization, in what specific areas does the imbalance occur?

◆ What does this heightened level of awareness to any imbalance mean to you as you look to the future of your organization?

◆ What do you need to do, as you look forward, to either gain or reset the balance of smarter and healthier in your organization?

These are important questions and fundamental considerations for you to ponder and address as we move deeper into the strategic business planning process.

"Your goals, minus your doubts, equals your reality."

Ralph Marston

DETERMINE YOUR STARTING POINT

In appraising your current realities, you have established an accurate set of what we call starting points for each area needing attention during the strategic planning process. You are instituting a set of measurable points, or baselines, emphasizing where you, your people, and your organization are. Once these points are acknowledged and plainly understood by all, you can use them as a reference point to assess and measure your forward progress toward your vision. Periodically reviewing your progress, or lack of progress, against these baselines is an important part of your strategic growth program.

The three Current Reality Assessment segments, when completed, provide the grounds for you and your Strategic Planning Team to move forward with accurate insights as you begin to wrestle with the real challenges and obstacles facing your organization. Dealing with the issues honestly and immediately will significantly affect your rate of forward progress.

"Our real problem, then, is not our strength today. It is rather the vital necessity of action today to ensure our strength tomorrow."

Dwight D. Eisenhower

Compare and contrast what you learned from these three elements of the Current Reality Assessment with the vision you created for yourself and your company in Chapter 3. Do this to determine if there is a gap between your current reality and your vision. This gap, if it exists, and the process we share to close the gap will be examined in Chapter 5.

ACTION INITIATORS

- ◆ Answer the EMT 33 questions, assessing the people, systems, and processes in your organization.
- ◆ Assess what your answers to the EMT 33 are telling you about yourself and your organization.
- ◆ Pinpoint areas for attention and improvement.
- ◆ Assess current key performance issues facing your organization. Check all the issues that apply to you and your organization.
- ◆ Select the top five and then the first of five issues facing you and your organization.
- ◆ Assess your current working environment.
- ◆ Identify areas in which your current working environment is not measuring up to the kind of organization you would like to have, or need to have, to support your vision for the future.
- ◆ Establish your baselines for judging future progress in the strategic business planning process and the healthy growth of your organization.

SECTION II
PREPARATION

5

THE GAP BETWEEN CURRENT REALITY AND VISION

"Don't tell me why you can't; tell me how you can."

Robert G. Ivanco

After you've established both your current reality and your vision for the future, you may have been struck by an observation that there is a distinct difference between where you are now and where you want to be, as defined by your vision. We call this difference the gap.

The important questions looming before you, now that you've taken the first two steps along the planning path, are these:

◆ What is the size of the gap between your current reality and your vision for the organization?

◆ Is the gap large or is it small?

◆ Is the gap manageable and bridgeable or do you look upon it as awesome, intimidating, and or overwhelming?

◆ What is your belief level in being able to find ways to effectively bridge the gap?

◆ Do you believe you have the people, the skills, the creativity, the resources, and the resolve to discover or invent ways to bridge the gap?

◆ Are you hopeful about bridging the gap?

◆ Fearful of not being able to bridge it?

If the prospect of bridging the gap has your pulse racing a bit, turn that fear and nervous energy into positive inertia and momentum—move forward and take action.

"Anything that I've done that ultimately was worthwhile . . . initially scared me to death."

Betty Bender

The minute you move past your fears, you triumph. And it's only the beginning of an exciting and energizing journey. William James, known to many as the father of American psychology, pointed out that there are three simple rules to follow if you *really* want to change your life:

◆ Start immediately.

◆ Do it flamboyantly.

◆ No exceptions.

To those three, add another:

◆ No excuses!

"You will never win if you never begin."

Robert H. Schuller

The processes outlined in the strategic growth program will help you extract all of the thoughts, ideas, and potential solutions you have begun creating. Using the methods we share with you in this book will allow you to begin considering a good many other important questions as well, about the future you'd like to see for yourself and your organization. All you need to do is take massive and immediate action now. Put yourself, your thoughts, and your instincts into immediate motion, with no further hesitation.

There is, with high probability, *nothing* in your life demanding that you hold back right now. There may be valid reasons to moderate the pace of your progress, yet there is no single appropriate reason to abstain from putting the leap in motion.

THE REALITIES IN BRIDGING THE GAP

The size of the gap you identify will play a large part in determining what exact steps you'll need to take to bridge it. How big is the leap you anticipate taking? Regardless of how near or vast the space may be in your gap, the first reality is a simple one: The bigger the gap, the longer it may take to move from where you are to where you want to be. A passionate sense of urgency is the strongest antidote to the first reality. That said, you are wise to recognize that deliberate, steady, measured progress, driven by urgent incremental action, will give you the greatest probability of reaching your desired destination in the shortest possible timeframe.

A second reality is that things will go wrong. Expecting the unexpected, while good advice, is not necessarily as easy to do as it sounds. Good, thorough planning can help, but there are other approaches that make good sense.

Turn this into an asset, not an obstacle. Reframe the impact that undesired and untimely appearances have on you and your team. You need to see the challenges, setbacks, and disappointments as opportunities to grow *beyond the growing pains* and sharpen yourselves with new knowledge, strengthened character, and valuable lessons learned. As Price Pritchett observes, "Failure can be a friend. There is a certain magic in mistakes. Problems, foul-ups, and breakdowns push you back on track, educate you, leaving you better equipped to navigate accurately towards your goal." Remember: When you're out there "pushing the envelope," unexpected reactions are likely to occur. Dealing with challenges will help you elevate your own game.

A third reality is that the greater the gap, the more potential distractions you'll encounter on the way to your vision. The path to your vision is loaded with distractive opportunities, and a larger gap allows more opportunity to sidetrack and divert you from your intended destination. Move forward like you're in the Indy 500—flat out, keep it on the track, off the walls, at all times. Stop only for quick, planned, timely, measured and well-orchestrated pit stops. Then hit the gas again.

"When it comes to the future, there are three kinds of people: those who let it happen; those who make it happen; and those who wonder what happened."

John M. Richardson Jr.

STEPS TO CLOSE THE GAP

Closing the gap is what your attention and efforts call for at this juncture. You and your team of leaders need straightforward, steady, planned, incremental progress, leading from your current reality toward your vision. The first step on your climb is to begin building on your strengths, both personally and as an organization, while you are offsetting or mitigating your weaknesses. Having taken an earlier inventory of the strengths and weaknesses of your organization during the Current Reality Assessment, as well as the full measure of the people in it, you are better prepared to know precisely whom you can depend on and whom you may need to replace. The initial push comes from the output of the Strategic Planning Team and the Strategic Planning Session. This is where the preliminary thrust is engaged and the heavy-lifting begins.

The second step is to manage and maneuver effectively through the maze of threats, obstacles, and opportunities that confront your organization. These are outlined and addressed in your strategic plan, even as it is evolving and being created. Although you may have a reasonably accurate picture emerging of the issues and obstacles facing you today, you will gain an even clearer appreciation for them during the Strategic Planning Session, as outlined in the next chapter. Clarity will come from the survey circulated earlier to key observers and participants, both inside and outside your organization. The survey should be compiled, and the information contained in the appraisal will provide valuable feedback and insights. As you emerge from the Strategic Planning Session and your plan is being researched and written, you will immediately begin the processes of executing agreed-upon solutions. You will begin implementing your actions well before the final written plan is completed.

The third step is to get into action: Work the plan, in all or in part, with an urgent aggressiveness. Execute, Execute, Execute!

The fourth step is to work to achieve your vision. As you near the vision, continue to establish the next meaningful levels of accomplishment and achievement.

"Only those who risk going too far can possibly find out how far one can go."

T.S. Eliot

KEEP YOUR EYE ON THE PRIZE, AND AVOID THE 14 TRAPS

After you've begun the process of closing the gap, you're likely to begin feeling impatient. You'll want to get to your destination without further delay. Although this impatience can be a good motivator, it can also be a source of painful irritation to yourself and those around you.

How long it takes to close the gap on your vision will in large part depend on—

◆ How well you and your team concentrate your efforts on progressing toward your goals and how well you execute on your individual and collective assignments

◆ How well you avoid common traps

These 14 traps are more barriers that you *must* confront to optimize your forward progress and momentum.

1. The *Be Reasonable* Trap—limiting your goals and aspirations to what you think you can have rather than what you want and need
2. The *Half Throttle* Trap—living life and approaching opportunities with a lukewarm level of desire and execution
3. The *More of the Same* Trap—reliance on trying harder, rather than on trying differently
4. The *Doubt* Trap—falling back on your perceived limits, rather than testing, besting, and resetting your limits
5. The *Faith in the Familiar* Trap—relying on old habits, routines, behaviors, and practices instead of trying new approaches
6. The *Methodology* Trap—being distracted by the means and losing sight of the goals

7. The *What I Can't See Isn't There* Trap—thinking you have to come up with all the solutions yourself, without the assistance of others
8. The *Playing It Safe* Trap—choosing to avoid risks altogether, or selecting the wrong risks to take
9. The *Passivity* Trap—wishing or hoping for what you want, while failing to take the appropriate actions that will turn wishes into results
10. The *Failures Aren't Allowed* Trap—rationalizing and equating failure as a sign that you should quit, give up the pursuit of your goals
11. The *Comfort Junkie* Trap—being afraid or unwilling to confront your fears and anxieties or perpetually remaining well inside your comfort zone
12. The *Use It or Lose It* Trap—not being willing to offer your gifts, your talents, and your abilities to the pursuit of organizational or personal goals
13. The *Perpetual Preparation* Trap—being bogged down and paralyzed by a perceived need to be perfectly prepared before any action can take place
14. The *Perfect Timing* Trap—waiting for the universe to align, the right set of circumstances to perfectly merge, before any action can be initiated

Do you see your behaviors mirrored in any of the 14 traps? If so, decide whether you're going to allow yourself to be trapped or whether you will use your new level of awareness to do something about it. It's up to you: Fall into the trap(s) or fight your way through them, turning excuses into extraordinary performance.

"Someone's sitting in the shade today because someone planted a tree a long time ago."

Warren Buffett

IDENTIFY STEPS AND TIMELINES FOR PROGRESS

How long will it take you to finish your strategic plan? How long will it take to begin getting the results you seek? How long will it take to get to the point where you achieve your vision? The answers will vary across a broad spectrum of potential responses. However, we have some general guidelines to share with you, drawn from our experience:

After you've held your Strategic Planning Session, you can begin immediately to research and commence writing the plan. Researching and writing the plan should be completed within 75 days.

You should begin executing the details of the plan immediately. As you wrap up the Strategic Planning Session, your action plans take shape and you assign the first round of due dates and completion deadlines.

The timelines to achieving your vision will depend on how far you wish to look; setting your vision. In the homebuilding industry, the average is a 5- to10-year vision and a 3- to 5-year Strategic Business Plan.

"Courage is fear holding on a minute longer."

George S. Patton

MAKE THE LEAP

It's up to you to make the leap and begin to close the gap. Are you ready to address these questions and act on the answers?

◆ Have you gotten tired of feeling stale, burned out, and in a rut?

◆ Have you grown weary under the weight of a life full of uninspiring repetition?

◆ Are you dissatisfied with your present level of performance and results, to the point you are prepared to do something *bold and aggressive* about it?

◆ Are you holding onto a dream of a much more satisfying future that you are not allowing yourself or granting yourself to pursue?

◆ Do you know of something really *big* you'd like to accomplish and are now ready to do?

◆ Can you identify something you *passionately* want?

◆ Are there signs of remarkable opportunities you can seize, which would re-energize you and your organization, setting up future success that you'd find satisfying?

If you begin to see a positive pattern emerge in your answers, it should provide you with the necessary spark to move into the Strategic Planning Session with passion, optimism, and high expectations, in turn igniting an infectious blaze of enthusiasm among all the participants. The next chapter outlines how to make the most of a Strategic Planning Session.

> *"Next in importance to having a good aim is to recognize when to pull the trigger."*
>
> *Elmer G. Letterman*

ACTION INITIATORS

◆ Determine the size of the gap between your current reality and your vision.
◆ Conclude whether or not you're ready to seek a quantum leap in performance for yourself and your organization.
◆ Understand and avoid the 14 traps.
◆ Prepare for the Strategic Planning Session, adopting the leadership mindset that will allow you to optimize the session experience and output for all participants.

6

PLANNING SESSION PREPARATION

"Confidence is contagious. So is lack of confidence."

Vince Lombardi

Most organizations allow *at least* a full, uninterrupted day for the Strategic Planning Session. If you've never completed a comprehensive Strategic Business Plan before, set aside another full day, or a couple of half-day sessions, to properly lay the foundation for the plan.

The first full day is the most important day of the process. It helps set the definitive tone and direction for the team, allows proper exposure to the emerging vision, and brings the planning team to common levels of communication, understanding, and full involvement in the process. A sample agenda that covers the full range of topics for a productive day one in the strategic planning process will look like Figure 6.1.

Follow-up sessions are scheduled to wrap up important group work, to continue educating the group in the planning process, and to wrestle with key performance issues, strategic and tactical considerations, and plan writing assignments.

"Thinking is the hardest work there is, which is probably why so few engage in it."

Henry Ford

SELECT THE STRATEGIC PLANNING TEAM

Selecting the Strategic Planning Team participants is a fairly straightforward process. The team should consist of:

1. Any and all active owners.
2. All members of your executive leadership team (e.g., the primary department leaders).
3. A select, representative group of staff members.

Keep in mind the optimum size for an effective Strategic Planning Session ranges from 6 to 10 participants. Smaller group sizes also can be productive and effective. Group sizes larger than 10 can also work, but expect the larger-sized groups to be less nimble and directable and more prone to slow down the session's momentum because of sheer group size, customary distractions, and conversational drift.

"Champions know that success is inevitable; there is no such thing as failure, only feedback. They know the best way to forecast the future is to create it."

Michael Gelb

FIGURE 6.1—SAMPLE AGENDA—STRATEGIC PLANNING SESSION

Universal Homes

DAY ONE AGENDA

Strategic Planning Session Agenda
Days, Dates & Times
8:00 AM to 5:00 PM

AM Session: 8:00 AM to 12:00 PM

Introductions, Session Purpose and Session Ground Rules.
Reviewing The Vision Process & Refining The Vision for Universal Homes.
The Top 5 and First of 5 Goal Setting Process.
Refining the Top 5 and First of 5 Goals for Universal Homes.
Determining Core Values for Universal Homes – The Mission to Mars.

12 Noon – 1:00 PM: Working Lunch

PM Session: 1:00 PM to 5:00 PM

Creating and Completing A Company Purpose Statement.
Creating Company Brand Promise & Core Values Statements.

Review Internal Strategic Planning Questionnaire Responses.

Identify The Key Performance Issues For Universal Homes.

Strengths	Leadership Team	Profitability & Financial Performance
Weaknesses	Sales & Marketing Team	Teamwork & Communication
Opportunities	Growth	Product/Service Development
Threats	Operations Team	Training & Development
Vulnerabilities	Market Needs	Customer Satisfaction & Resources

Identify Short and Intermediate-Term Key Performance Goals For Universal Homes.
Prioritize and Determine Sequencing for each Issues Area.

"Take the Pulse" on Day One Progress and Participant Satisfaction
Set the Stage for An Extremely Productive Day Two

5:00 PM – ADJOURN

DAY TWO AGENDA

AM Session: 8:00 AM to 12:00 PM

Building The Universal Homes Strategic Growth Plan

Conduct Key Performance Issues Consulting Process on ALL Key Issues
Learning & Using The Hoshin Method of Problem Solving.

Strengths, Weaknesses, Opportunities, Threats, and Vulnerabilities.

KPI's: Leadership Team, Sales & Marketing, Growth, Operations, Market Positioning
Financial Performance & Profitability, Productivity, Quality & Quality Control,
Accounting Information, Teamwork & Communication, Products & Services, Training
Development, Customer Satisfaction, and Resources.

Prioritize Key Performance Issues affecting Current, Intermediate, & Long-Term Results
Develop Goals, Action Steps, Commitments and Deadlines.

12 Noon – 1:00 PM: Working Lunch

PM Session: 1:00 PM to 5:00 PM

Refining The Universal Homes Strategic Growth Plan

1:00 –4:30 PM

Continue and Complete KPI Consulting Process on ALL Key Performance Issues

Identify Key Universal Homes Critical Numbers for Balance of Plan Period
Develop & Agree On Key Performance Benchmarks and Goals.

4:30 PM: Wrap-up

Develop, Review, Refine, and Assign Key Performance Issues Action Accountabilities
Develop, Review, Refine, and Assign Accountabilities for Writing 2003-2007 Strategic
Plan.

Clarify Next Required Actions & Accountabilities.
Set Dates For Next Follow-up Meeting(s).

Complete Checkpoint Comment and Momentum Surveys: Measure Client Satisfaction

5:00 PM - ADJOURN

FIGURE 6.1 (CON'T)

EMT Client Strategic Planning Session Survey Questions

Vision

■ Its 5 years from now. Our Organization has become:

■ What OBSTACLES must our Organization overcome between now and 5 years from now to ensure our success?

Mission/Purpose

■ As you understand it, our Organization's Mission/Purpose includes the following elements:

■ Our Organization's Mission/Purpose, going forward, should <u>also</u> include the following elements:

■ To successfully complete its Mission/Purpose, our Organization needs to:

Core Values

■ The CURRENT Core Values of our Organization right now are:

■ The Core Values we need to acquire as we go forward are:

Strengths

■ The Greatest Strengths of our Organization <u>right now</u> are:

Weaknesses

■ The Greatest Weaknesses of our Organization <u>right now</u> are:

Opportunities

■ The Greatest Opportunities for our Organization <u>right now</u> are:

Threats and Vulnerabilities

■ The Greatest Threats and Vulnerabilities for our Organization <u>right now</u> are:

GATHER THE STRATEGIC PLANNING SURVEY

Feedback is one of the hardest things a person must face, either in personal life or in a career. The same can be said for businesses and organizations. Our environments are so often full of negative feedback and negative reinforcement that feedback is something many outright dread. Feedback is particularly painful to endure when it is perceived to be critical of us as an individual, of our professional performance, or of our organization's performance. People often take any and all feedback personally, believing it reflects their efforts individually. Feedback is heat we'd rather not withstand, given the choice. So it is no small surprise that many individuals and organizations, particularly those with a measure of dysfunction in their culture, look upon surveys of employee attitude and input as a reckless, dangerous, and excruciatingly painful chase. Fearful of what they might learn from the survey and from their own people, an organization may believe that ignorance and denial are much easier to tolerate than any dose of the truth.

Although feedback can be viewed, depending on your perspective, as positive, neutral, or negative in nature, the one thing it always turns out to be is *essential*. Like it or not, regardless of your tolerance for hearing the truth you need to know how people are thinking *and* feeling about how you are meeting their needs, the needs of your customers, and the needs of your market. Hearing the truth helps you and your planning team—

◆ Make better-informed decisions

◆ Understand where the real issues and impediments are located

◆ Comprehend the magnitude and the impact of problems

◆ Ask better questions that add to your knowledge base

With these thoughts in mind, one of the most important elements of the strategic growth program and the strategic business planning process is to gather input from our customers, both internal and external. Internal customers are employees or staff members in our organization, from the most elementary entry-level position to the person(s) at the top. External customers consist of every key relationship we have as we conduct our business, including our customers, vendors, suppliers, partners, trade contractors, and regulatory agency staff. Everybody's opinion counts, and everyone's input is valued and welcome. The strategic planning survey formally seeks the input of internal and external sources.

> *"You win not by chance, but by preparation."*
>
> *Roger Maris*

THE VALUE OF AN INTERNAL STRATEGIC PLANNING SURVEY

The internal strategic planning survey is a document that should be prepared and circulated by a neutral and trustworthy person. This person should have stature with the respondents sufficient to encourage a full and truthful disclosure of what is in every respondent's heart and mind.

You should circulate a minimum of 8 to 12 surveys internally, and cap the number of distributed surveys at a total of 20. Fifteen internal surveys is an ideal number for most organizations. With an ideal target of 12 to 15 survey responses, the patterns, trends, and messages in the compiled internal survey document generally will be fresh and manageable. Good ideas stand out, while dominant themes and significant issues emerge effortlessly.

Usually accompanied by a cover letter highlighting the importance of the survey to the strategic planning process, the survey is circulated with a return due date about two weeks after it is initially sent to each of the selected participants. This allows sufficient time for participants to fully think through their answers, to the point that the answers are complete, thoughtful, and meticulous in representing the views and opinions of each respondent.

GATHER VALID INTERNAL INPUT: INTERNAL SURVEY QUESTIONS

When you compile an internal strategic planning survey, solicit responses in an open-ended fashion. You want to persuade participants to share their unadulterated perceptions and passions across a large landscape of thought-provoking questions. The surveys circulated internally for the strategic planning process can be selected from both lists of standard questions and customized inquiries for clients. Numbering from as few as 10 to as many as 37 questions, the surveys usually look similar to Figures 6.2 and 6.3.

Selecting the right questions for your internal survey is simply a matter of sitting down and determining which questions allow you to uncover the answers and awareness that are most important for you and your business. You don't need to use all of these questions if you believe your slate of respondents lacks the time or the inclination to fill out a lengthy survey. Your goal is to encourage the respondents to provide you with as much insight as possible so that you can make better decisions, accounting for their needs and interests, within your strategic planning framework.

If you cannot find all the right questions from among those listed above, develop customized questions. Begin by asking yourself, "What is it, specifically, I would like to know?" The major pitfall of developing survey questions comes from phrasing a question in a non-neutral way that leads respondents to tell you what they believe you want to hear instead of honest feedback. Remember, your goal in designing customized survey questions is to get the truth.

GATHER THE EXTERNAL STRATEGIC PLANNING SURVEY

As with our internal survey, we want to encourage each respondent in the external strategic planning survey to share what they see and how they feel about a range of issues. Again, you want your external customers to share their pure and unvarnished perceptions across a much smaller backdrop of thought-provoking questions designed to deliver the insights and truths needed to render superior thinking and healthier decisions.

Always accompanied by a cover letter highlighting the importance of the survey to the strategic planning process, the external survey is circulated with a return due date of, again, about two weeks after it is sent to the selected participants. This allows sufficient time for each participant to speedily, yet completely, think through answers and respond in a thoughtful manner.

"Everything should be as simple as possible, but not simpler."

Albert Einstein

EXTERNAL SURVEY QUESTIONS

Keep the surveys produced for clients in the strategic planning process simple. Combine a mix of both numerical ratings and open-ended input from respondents, while still allowing for customized, targeted inquiries for clients. In the interest of keeping things uncomplicated, your external survey can consist of four standard survey questions. The external survey questions usually look similar to those in Figure 6.4.

SELECT THE STRATEGIC PLANNING SESSION LEADER

The reasons to contract a qualified, seasoned, and knowledgeable facilitator for your session are many.

◆ An outside facilitator can bring neutrality and objectivity to the proceedings, which are difficult to secure if all of the session participants are affiliated with the organization in any way.

◆ An accomplished facilitator can bring new ideas and approaches to the table, which may allow participants to develop new perceptions, innovative thoughts, and breakthroughs in belief and comprehension.

FIGURE 6.2—INTERNAL STRATEGIC PLANNING SURVEY

<u>Predominant Frustrations</u>

- Your predominant frustrations with our organization *right now* are:

- Resolving your predominant frustrations would produce what positive results?

<u>Greatest Fears</u>

- The greatest fears you have for our organization *right now*, if any, are:

<u>To Increase Sales and Profitability</u>

- If you were responsible for increasing sales revenues and profitability at our organization *right now*, what would you do to ensure success from your efforts?

<u>Continue / Start / Stop</u>

- In the next 12 months, our organization should CONTINUE:

- In the next 12 months, our organization should START:

- In the next 12 months, our organization should STOP:

<u>To Become A Better Place To Work</u>

- To make our organization an even better and more satisfying place to work, it should:

<u>To Help Us Better Do Our Jobs</u>

- To help us do our jobs even better and become more successful, our organization should:

<u>Essential Communication to Ownership or Management</u>

- What else, if anything, would you like to communicate to ownership or management in our organization at this time?

FIGURE 6.3—INTERNAL STRATEGIC PLANNING SURVEY

Key Performance Issues Analysis At Our Organization

Key performance issues are defined as:
"Issues that, if properly addressed, are crucial to optimizing our individual or organizational performance and ensuring the health & longevity of our organization."

- Key performance issues facing or affecting our *leadership team* at our organization:

- Key performance issues facing us in *sales and marketing* at our organization:

- Key performance issues facing us in terms of *growth* at our organization:

- Key performance issues in *operations* at our organization:

- Key performance issues in *market positioning or targeting* at our organization:

- Key performance issues in *financial performance and profitability* at our organization:

- Key performance issues in *productivity* at our organization:

- Key performance issues in *quality & quality control* at our organization:

- Key performance issues in *accounting information for decision making* at our organization:

- Key performance issues affecting *teamwork and communication* at our organization:

- Key performance issues in *products, services, and product/service development* at our organization:

- Key performance issues in *training and development* at our organization:

- Key performance issues affecting *customer satisfaction* at our organization:

- Key performance issues in terms of *equipment & tools* at our organization:

- Key performance issues in terms of *information technology or technology tools* at our organization:

- Key performance issues in terms of *required resources* at our organization:

◆ A skilled facilitator may be able to take you much farther, faster, than you could proceed on your own.

FIGURE 6.4—EXTERNAL STRATEGIC PLANNING SURVEY

EMT External Client—Strategic Planning Session Survey

Your Level of Satisfaction With Our Business Relationship

■ Rate your level of satisfaction with our business relationship today.

1	2	3	4	5
Low	Needs Work	Okay	Good	The Best

What must happen to make it a "5"?

Satisfaction With Our Customer Service

■ Rate your level of satisfaction with our customer service today.

1	2	3	4	5
Low	Needs Work	Okay	Good	The Best

What must happen to make it a "5"?

Satisfaction With Our Products and/or Services

■ Rate your level of satisfaction with our products and/or services today.

1	2	3	4	5
Low	Needs Work	Okay	Good	The Best

What must happen to make it a "5"?

Satisfaction With Our Overall Performance

■ Rate your level of satisfaction with our overall performance today.

1	2	3	4	5
Low	Needs Work	Okay	Good	The Best

What must happen to make it a "5"?

◆ The right facilitator can energize your planning team as a source of fresh, inspirational leadership, adding a new dimension and personality to your existing mix of players.

The above are all legitimate reasons for engaging an outside facilitator, but there are several valid reasons to forego such a commitment.

◆ You (or someone else on your staff) possess the skills and experience to conduct an effective strategic planning process and can be comfortably neutral and objective.

◆ You believe that the facilitators available to you do not have the level of experience or skill necessary to lead your strategic planning processes that you or your people possess.

◆ You don't believe the expenditure for an outside facilitator will produce an acceptable rate of return for the fees charged, and you are better off investing the funds in some other, more beneficial manner.

◆ You simply don't have the cash to invest.

"Start with what is right, rather than what is acceptable."

Fyodor Dostoevsky

SELECT THE RIGHT SITE

There are a many items to consider when selecting the right site for your Strategic Planning Session. Some considerations include—

◆ Does the site cost fit within the budget?

◆ Is the location convenient for all participants?

◆ Are the site services and amenities correct for your needs?

◆ Is food and beverage service available on-site or nearby?

◆ Does the site meet your customary standards?

◆ Is the atmosphere conducive to optimal productivity for your session?

◆ Is it quiet enough to allow for concentration and thoughtful reflection?

◆ Is it secure enough that you will likely not run into competitors?

When selecting a site, consider the full spectrum of available options.

◆ Local conference centers

◆ Customary hotel and motel meeting facilities

◆ Local libraries

◆ School facilities

◆ Municipally sponsored services

One common denominator is that all of the above potential sites are off-premises, away from the distractions and interruptions of the daily business routine. There is real value in taking people away from the full range of mental disruptions that can occur around the office.

Although we strongly recommend that you avoid staying on-site, it makes sense to use your own office facilities if it turns out to be the best match for the session's needs.

CREATE THE RIGHT ATMOSPHERE

The Strategic Planning Session is supposed to be highly interactive, with open discussion and healthy conflict taking place about important issues. Important decisions should be reached in a concordant and cooperative manner. As Patrick Lencioni explains in his book, *The Obsessions of an Extraordinary Executive: The Four Disciplines at the Heart of Making Any Organization World Class*, the right kind of environment and atmosphere for a successful strategic planning environment encourages cohesive teambuilding, creates trust, eliminates politics, and increases organizational efficiencies by—

◆ Knowing and coming to terms with one another's unique strengths and weaknesses, as well as those of your organization

◆ Openly engaging in constructive ideological conflict

◆ Holding one another accountable for behaviors and actions

◆ Committing to group decisions, both during and coming out of the planning session

The elements listed above are essential in creating an organization that is healthy, smart, and productive. They generate a Strategic Planning Session that is dynamic, energizing, and rewarding for all participants. As the leader and initiator of the strategic planning processes within your organization, it is in your interest to encourage these qualities in your planning session.

"I determined never to stop until I had come to the end and achieved my purpose."

David Livingstone

OPTIMIZE THE STRATEGIC PLANNING SESSION EXPERIENCE

To get the most out of your Strategic Planning Session, keep in mind the following steps both during and immediately after the session.

During the session—

◆ Keep the session upbeat and positive, moving briskly on track, in-sync with the agenda, and making visibly evident progress for all to acknowledge.

◆ Have someone assigned to scribe a record of all decisions, accountabilities, and due date commitments advanced throughout the session.

◆ Capture and detail the content of all discussions, conclusions, and production thoroughly during the session.

◆ Retain copies of all charts and all other diagrams or meaningful visual output from any and all breakout meetings.

Following the session—

◆ Prepare a written report to circulate to all appropriate staff members, detailing the progress and output of the session.

◆ Schedule and conduct a one- or two-hour meeting with all staff members to share the updated and final version of the vision and the written report in detail; explain the decisions and action commitments that were made during the Strategic Planning Session; answer any questions the group may have for members of the planning team; and chart the course and timeframes for future progress.

By following these simple recommended steps, at the conclusion of the Strategic Planning Session you can significantly leverage and magnify the benefits of your efforts.

ACTION INITIATORS

◆ Determine whether you will conduct your Strategic Planning Session in a single day, over two consecutive days, or over a multitude of shorter days.
◆ Set a date for your Strategic Planning Session.
◆ Select and reserve the proper site for your Strategic Planning Session.
◆ Develop and finalize a Strategic Planning Session agenda.
◆ Select the participating members of your Strategic Planning Team.
◆ Develop and circulate an internal strategic planning survey.
◆ Develop and circulate an external strategic planning survey.
◆ Collect all strategic planning survey responses by the designated due date.
◆ Compile the survey responses into a bound report, to share with your Strategic Planning Team.
◆ Conduct your Strategic Planning Session on the designated date.
◆ Capture and retain all output from the session.
◆ Schedule and conduct an all-organization meeting to share the vision, the details of the Strategic Planning Session, and the course of future strategic planning efforts and activities.

7

VISION, MISSION, AND BRAND PROMISE

"High expectations are the key to everything."

Sam Walton

One of the most important opening elements of the Strategic Planning Session is sharing the vision you created with the rest of your leadership team. Allow them to explore, examine, and comment upon the vision. By doing so, the finished document will reflect the interests and the input of the entire team. Also share the full spectrum of the top 5 and first of 5 goals you developed for the organization.

REFINE THE VISION

Walk your planning team carefully through a full reading of the vision. Read each paragraph aloud, having each of the planning team members take turns verbalizing the vision. Allow the words to echo throughout the meeting room. At the end of each paragraph, encourage a discussion. Openly solicit their responses by asking—

◆ How do you feel about what you've just heard?

◆ Does it ring true?

◆ Does it seem doable? Is it achievable?

◆ Would you make any changes to this paragraph in the vision? If so, what might the changes include?

◆ Are there ways to make the paragraph content and message even stronger and more compelling?

◆ Can you personally support this aspect of our vision, before we move forward to the next paragraph?

Listen carefully to the responses. Study individual and collective body language throughout the reading of your vision document for signs of either acceptance or rejection of the message. Are people on your team "buying into" what they are reading and hearing? Is the reception enthusiastic, lukewarm, or absent entirely? Is there support to move forward and actively pursue the vision? Does each paragraph and the entire vision pass "the snicker factor"—not laughed at in either uncomfortable, ridiculing, or unsupportive ways? As the author of the vision, these are the signs you are assessing and the questions you are asking yourself and evaluating throughout the reading of the draft vision.

"To avoid criticism, do nothing, say nothing, be nothing."

Albert Green Hubbard

If your team is responding favorably and enthusiastically to the vision document, you are on the right track. Yet even in light of receiving positive, supportive responses, keep asking the difficult questions. In many cases, this will be the first substantive exposure your vision will have to the audience with a significant interest in its practical implementation and who will likely end up carrying most of the burden of its execution. Take their reactions seriously, and be prepared to adjust and modify your vision in response to the perceptive, heartfelt input from your leadership team.

> *"The meaning of life is to give meaning to life."*
>
> *Ken Hudgins*

ENCOURAGE LEADERSHIP TEAM TO IMPROVE THE VISION

The key to leaving the Strategic Planning Session with a fully aligned leadership team, eager to begin the work of turning the vision into reality, is allowing a transfer of ownership to occur during the reading and examination of the vision. This will take place from the original authors of the document to all members of the Strategic Planning Team. This transition in ownership occurs by having the original authors release exclusive creative claims to the vision while exhibiting a vigorous level of objectivity as they encourage and evaluate all the diverse input from the planning team. Given well-meaning and constructive input, objective evaluation by the original authors provides the means to strengthen and improve the vision. This objectivity creates an avalanche of decisive support from the entire leadership team that builds in intensity throughout the Strategic Planning Session.

To encourage this transition in ownership, make sure each participant is invited and encouraged to participate fully in both reading the vision and contributing comments on each aspect of the vision. Actively facilitate and promote the sharing of opinions, respectfully considering every participant's input.

> *"Most people are about as happy as they make up their minds to be."*
>
> *Abraham Lincoln*

IDENTIFY CORPORATE VALUES

Central to the process of perusing the vision is the agreement on corporate values, core beliefs, organizational aspirations, and benchmark outcomes that key people in your organization can support. Areas you will want to explore and clarify include:

◆ How will you conduct yourselves, as you conduct your business?

◆ What are the standards you set for yourselves and strive to achieve?

◆ What will you hold sacred?

◆ Whose behavior and performance will be modeled, emulated, and celebrated throughout the organization?

◆ To what levels of character will you aspire, both individually and collectively?

◆ What outcomes will be considered worthy of the required effort?

◆ How will you ultimately define success from your sacrifices, contributions, and efforts?

These are important considerations for the entire Strategic Planning Team to confront and clarify. It needs to be complete before you move forward.

If the owners have done a thorough job of thinking these questions through in their early initial draft of the vision, it will be easier to move through and gain consensus and concordant agreement among the entire team. However, be forewarned that this portion of the strategic planning process is often the point at which the greatest level of dissonance and disagreement can occur. If there are fundamental philosophical differences as to *how* the organization should act and behave as it conducts its business, or if questions of ethics, integrity, and tactical execution practices are raised, heated exchanges may arise. Sometimes these exchanges can be extremely healthy in the process.

One of the best ways to cut quickly to the core of your values and beliefs, desired behaviors and virtues, and worthy intentions is to engage the Strategic Planning Team in a simple exercise called *Mission to Mars*. If you've ever been through the laborious, agonizing experience of defining values and core beliefs with another company on your way up to your present position, it may well have taken a long time, might have cost a lot of money, and may possibly have ended up producing a finished document that failed to capture the exact essence of the unique culture in which you found yourself at the time. Yes, it got the job done, but if it failed to capture the *soul* of your company or organization, it failed.

Using the *Mission to Mars* method allows a smart, healthy company to produce a solid first draft of their core beliefs and values in 15 minutes or less *and* construct an inspiring and candid document that captures the *soul* of the organization, in usually an hour or less. How does it work? With your Strategic Planning Team, try this:

◆ Ask the group to pretend they are a distinguished team of alien Martian anthropologists studying earthly business practices, and they are trying to understand your own organization's inimitable culture.

◆ Each alien anthropologist is to select the names of five employees of your organization—*ones not in the room*—who will be selected to participate in an exchange study and will travel to Mars for further first-hand observation.

◆ Each of the Martian anthropologists speaks no earthly languages, certainly *not* English, and all have lost the ability to read the ancient universal language of the cosmos called PowerPoint. So whatever the Martians learn about your organization's culture, they will gain purely from their own powers of direct observation.

◆ Given these limitations, which five employees from your company would best convey to the Martians what is good and valued within your organization, that contributes instrumentally to its *soul*? Which five would you select as most worthy to give you and your other Martian colleagues the best sense of what makes your organization a potent, competitive universal powerhouse in the cosmos?

◆ When each Martian anthropologist has five names selected, have each Martian scholar voice the selections. At this point, do not ask *why* they selected their individual choices. Simply record the names and tally the total number of times each name presented is mentioned. Then identify the names of the three to five employees mentioned most often. (*The Martian scholars must agree to keep this listing **strictly confidential** The List should not leave the room and should be destroyed after this exercise.*)

◆ Starting with the employee who received the most mentions, initiate a healthy conversation about each of these individuals. Questions you might want to ask may include:

  ◆ Who are they?

  ◆ What makes them unique?

  ◆ How do they go about their work?

  ◆ What would customers and co-workers say about them?

  ◆ Why are they important and/or valuable to the organization?

◆ What do they contribute that ensures a positive working environment?

◆ What actions describe their positive conduct and productive behaviors?

◆ Record the answers on a chart board. As you begin recording what is said, patterns and themes will begin to emerge. You will likely realize the words, possibly less polished or descriptive at first, become more and more reflective of the true perception and unique culture of your business. Remember: The goal of your Martian anthropologists is to observe and capture the quintessence of these earthly all-stars, as they represent *the very best* your organization has to offer and reflect your very own core values and sustainable operational beliefs.

◆ As you continue refining and massaging the input from the exercise the right words will mysteriously emerge. The right words will appear and begin to inexplicably sort themselves out. Your employees will start voicing some of your own deeply held beliefs, motivations, and favorite phrases, adopting them as if they themselves owned or authored them. Then it quickly rolls into a process of simple word-smithing, hammering out a massive yield of ideas in the form of key words, phrases, and principals that you can all adopt and believe in going forward.

The *Mission to Mars* exercise is a lot of fun and can be very powerful in aligning the entire Strategic Planning Team around the core beliefs and values that make up your organization. You will discover a vigorous blending of attitudes, beliefs, and values occurring through this component of the process. The leadership team experiences an enhanced level of bonding and alignment, while reciprocated degrees of understanding emerge. Does this have value to you and to your organization? Without a doubt! In the absence of such alignment, an organization can weaken and wander in times of challenge and difficulty. In the presence of such alignment, however, an organization's strength makes it resilient, sturdy, and virtually bullet-proof.

What do the core beliefs and values look like and sound like coming out of the process? As Jim Collins, who co-authored the book *Built to Last,* puts it:

> "*. . . there is no universally right set of core values. A company need not have as its core value customer service (Sony doesn't) or respect for the individual (Disney doesn't) or quality (Wal-Mart doesn't) or market focus (Hewlett Packard doesn't) or teamwork (Nordstrom doesn't). A company might have operating practices and business strategies around those qualities without having them at the essence of its being. Furthermore, great companies need not have likeable or humanistic core values, although many do. The key is not what core values an organization has, but that it has core values at all.*"

Some examples of core values and beliefs, drawn from several different companies, end up being tailored to the distinctive culture of the organization. For Gazelles, these core values and beliefs consist of six elements.

◆ Practice what we preach

◆ Produce ecstatic customers

◆ First class for less

◆ Honor intellectual capitalists

◆ Everyone an entrepreneur

◆ Never, ever, ever give up

For executive mentors and trainers, the core values and beliefs also consist of six elements.

◆ Maintain the highest ethical, moral, and service standards.

◆ Offer the most objective, experienced, and knowledgeable insights, advice, and guidance at all times.

◆ Provide comprehensive, sensible, cost-effective solutions to our clients.

◆ Emphasize the important balance between relationships and results.

◆ Hold the answers within yourselves. Facilitate the answers out, for all to see and hear.

◆ Do whatever it takes to ensure each and every client's needs are met and their expectations exceeded.

McArthur Homes, in South Jordan, Utah, determined that their core values and beliefs consist of eight key components.

◆ Care for customers

◆ Completely reliable

◆ Thick-skinned, hard-working, and team-oriented

◆ Calming in the face of conflict

◆ Honesty and integrity above all

◆ Organized, dedicated, smart, and humble

◆ Open and speak your mind in plain terms

◆ Always helpful

Campbell Companies in Colorado Springs, Colorado, determined that their core values and beliefs consist of nine key statements.

◆ We can compete with anyone in our industry and come out on top.

◆ We exercise wise and prudent caution in the marketplace, carefully calculating our level of risk and reward.

◆ Our passion for our business is apparent to everyone with whom we interact in our daily business dealings.

◆ We make a difference in our community, by offering exceptional opportunities to those seeking to better their lives.

◆ Everybody counts!

◆ We speak openly and honestly to everyone at all times.

◆ No one is perfect among us. We all make mistakes. We are all works-in-progress.

◆ We meet our goals. When we fail to do so, we know the reasons and take immediate corrective action.

◆ We deliver on our promises and commitments.

As you can see, each of these expressions of core values and beliefs is different, yet each conveys a distinctive snapshot of the operational attitudes and philosophies at the core of *how* each of these businesses wishes to conduct its affairs in their respective communities and markets. Yet all serve to define and sculpt the qualities that allow an organization to be itself and serve to explicitly distinguish what is most important to a group of owners and leaders in the way they seek their success.

> *"The thing you really believe in always happens . . .*
> *and the belief in a thing makes it happen."*
>
> Frank Lloyd Wright

BUILD SUPPORT FOR THE VISION

As you put the finishing touches on the vision, prior to rolling it out to the larger audience in your organization you want to ensure that the final vision reflects the collective input of everyone on the Strategic Planning Team. Conduct one final pass around the room, asking each participant to take a few minutes to review what has been shared and expressed during the lengthy review of the draft vision document. Then ask each person these four questions:

◆ Is there anything that you believe still needs to be changed in this vision?

◆ Are there any concerns you have about this vision, as we've updated it?

◆ What do you like BEST about the updated vision?

◆ Is this a vision you can fully support?

If you've done a fine job of cultivating and sharing your vision with your planning staff and have incorporated their comments and concerns successfully into your updated vision, you'll find the level of infectious support that builds during these rounds of questions to be gratifying and energizing. Simply ask each person the four questions listed above. Build on their positive responses. Explore any lack of enthusiasm. Take a clear reading. And facilitate the creation of cohesion, alignment, commitment, and passionate support for the latest evolution of the vision before moving forward.

> *"I know quite certainly that I myself have no special talent; curiosity, obsession, and*
> *dogged endurance, combined with self-criticism, have brought me to my ideas."*
>
> Albert Einstein

ESTABLISH MISSION AND PURPOSE

What are the differences between mission and purpose? There really are no differences between the two. For your application, the terms are interchangeable in the strategic planning process. The mission or purpose statement is designed to capture, in concise, carefully selected words or phrases, precisely why your organization is doing what it has chosen to do; why the destination is important in your vision; what higher principles drive the actions and behaviors of your organization; and why you have such enthusiasm and dedication for what you're seeking in terms of success.

If the values and core beliefs are the soul of the organization, the mission and purpose form its heart, while the strategic plan serves as the brain and nervous system. The mission and purpose helps an organization understand what's really important as it conducts its business.

This mission and purpose statement format addresses four separate building blocks:

◆ Profile

◆ Method

◆ Specific outcomes

◆ Measurement criteria

In addressing each of the four building blocks, there are some uncomplicated guidelines to help direct your creative efforts.

◆ In settling on a profile of *who you are* and *what you do*, you're describing your organization in 15 seconds or less. Use active verbs, such as "building, creating, planning, coordinating, designing, constructing, growing, satisfying, delivering."

◆ In crafting your response on the method of *how you do what you do*, detail the methods and values you'll employ and apply, emphasizing the qualities you'll utilize to drive and direct your efforts.

◆ As to *specific outcomes,* you want to unequivocally detail, in unambiguous terms, the specific outcomes you are looking to create through your efforts.

◆ *Measurement criteria* requires you to state the specific evidence, indicators, or criteria that will ultimately signify your success or failure in attaining your mission and purpose.

So what might a mission and purpose statement look like? The following mission and purpose statement reflects all four of the building blocks cited above.

"We are creating, designing, and delivering a powerful and effective accelerated leadership growth program for delivery to carefully selected, high potential leaders and managers within Trammell Crow Company and other appropriate organizations, by October 1st of 2000, in a collaborative way that utilizes our considerable experience, diverse talents and perspectives, proven processes, and our depth of human relationship and leadership coaching skills.
Our Program participants will

1. Learn about leadership and management trends and tools and how to apply the approaches and processes within their organizations;
2. Understand their individual leadership and management styles, strengths, and their potential for future professional growth and development, as well as those of their colleagues;
3. Receive valuable feedback from their colleagues and other program participants, to use in developing goals and plans for accelerating both personal and professional growth; and
4. Gain insights and tool sets that allow each participant to chart a course toward improved professional productivity and a more balanced, fulfilling, and satisfying life.

Our success is measured by the level of participant satisfaction, as captured and expressed in post-program surveys, and by the degree to which participants implement and execute the concepts, processes, tools, and techniques of the accelerated leadership growth program. Supportive evidence will include measurable improvements in operational and financial performance and quantifiable shifts in perceived professional effectiveness and personal life balance for each participant."

For this particular project, who they are and what they're doing, how they're going about doing it, what their desired outcomes are, and how they're going to measure success is very clear in the above example. It leaves little to the imagination for anyone involved in the project.

By applying these four elementary building blocks to the development of your organization's mission and purpose, you'll be able to define the details that communicate the essential direction, style, destinations, and outcomes you seek.

"Strength is a matter of the made up mind."

John Beecher

ESTABLISH BRAND PROMISE

Brand promise is the commitment an organization makes to itself, to its customers and clients, and to the markets it serves to satisfy the key needs of its customers, clients, and chosen markets, in measurable terms. Brand promise also has been described as an organization's value-added proposition, or market differentiator. Brand promise is the quantifiable means by which an organization guides, evaluates, and confirms delivery of products or services that satisfy the needs of customers, clients, vendors, and all the other important relationships it must serve in the successful conduct of its business.

A successfully defined brand promise targets those needs that are really important to your customers. It pinpoints those needs that bring customers to you and keeps them coming back for more of what your business offers. Your brand promise is the dominant factor that distinctively separates you from the competition. Brand promise is the foundation, often the cornerstone, from which all important leadership decisions are made.

The essentials of defining your brand promise are likely already waiting for you to awaken them and give them life, with roots doubtlessly located somewhere within your vision, your top 5 and first of 5 goals, and your mission and purpose statement. To uncover it, ask yourself, "What is our customer's greatest need?" What you're searching for is the answer to this question. What is it that your customers *need*—not want— that they are having difficulty receiving or obtaining and which your organization, better than any other, can provide? When you are able to determine your customer's dominant need and establish how and why you and your organization can satisfy that need in the most effective, expeditious, and exemplary manner, you will have your brand promise.

If you find yourself still struggling with the creation of your brand promise after you've spent some quality time and effort, there's another tool you can turn to. By answering the following value-add questions, you can close the gap on completing your own brand promise. The value-add questions include:

◆ What is your biggest, most exciting long-term goal for your organization?

◆ How do you define your geographical markets, your product lines, and your channels of distribution?

◆ What is the biggest *need* your customers have, as distinguished from their *wants?*

◆ What bottlenecks, obstacles, shortages, or chokepoints exist within your chosen market or industry, and how might you best overcome them or control them?

◆ What decisive competitive advantages might you gain from utilizing and applying leading-edge technologies to best meet your customer's needs?

REFINE VISION, MISSION AND PURPOSE, AND BRAND PROMISE

Before moving on to the next element in the Strategic Planning Session, here are some tips about completing the final version of your vision, mission and purpose, and brand promise and preparing them for presentation by the rest of your organization. First of all, there comes a point when you need to quit tinkering and refining the vision draft and turn it into a final vision.

ROLL OUT THE VISION, MISSION AND PURPOSE, AND BRAND PROMISE

Within a few days of completing the Strategic Planning Session, schedule and conduct an immediate meeting with the balance of your organization's staff. Having not been directly involved in your session, they will likely be curious about what you've been working on and about what has developed from the strategic planning effort. They'll also want to know the impact the vision and the strategic plan will have on them. Quite simply: They want, and need, to be informed and involved.

The meeting should be a celebration of hard work and worthy outcomes. The tone should be positive, constructive, enthusiastic, and upbeat. It can be built around a company luncheon or barbecue. Regardless of when, or where, or how it is held, the meeting often represents a turning point for an organization. You are no longer flying solely by the seat of your pants. You have a vision for the future. And a plan is coming along to turn that vision into a reality. So it's no longer a question of where you're going or how you're going to get there. You have a clear idea of where you're headed and what challenges you're going to be facing along the way. Fewer surprises. Greater security. Confidence as you face your future. That's what this meeting can communicate, and produce, for you and your organization.

The meeting should cover several major points as you present your Strategic Planning Session output to your staff.

◆ Read through the vision in its entirety.

◆ Allow for questions and solicit responses from the assembled staff members. Once again, ask the all-important questions:

　◆ How do you feel about what you've just heard?

　◆ Does it ring true, to you?

　◆ Does it seem doable? Is it achievable?

　◆ Would you make any changes to this paragraph in the vision? If so, what might they include?

　◆ Are there ways to make the paragraph content and message even stronger and more compelling?

　◆ Can you personally support this aspect of our vision, before we move forward to the next paragraph?

◆ Review the top 5 and first of 5 goals for each of the specified time periods. Take the pulse of the attendees: Doable? Exciting? Energizing? Worthy?

◆ Review the mission and purpose. Explain the rationale behind the statement. Solicit input and comments. Seek approval of the statement from the attendees.

◆ Review the brand promise. Clarify the grounds upon which the brand promise was born. Answer questions. Request additional comments or observations from the attending staff. Validate the level of support, or lack thereof, for the brand promise.

◆ Conclude the session with a commitment from the leader of the strategic planning process to continue closing in on a written strategic plan that will serve to deliver the organization to the vision you've just reviewed, in all of its elements.

This is a meeting that will last from one to two hours, depending on the size of the group. Regardless of length, this is an opportunity for you and your planning team to put your work on full display and for you to collectively convey to your entire organization the positive feelings and expectations you carried away from the Strategic Planning Session. Make the most of this opportunity to light a huge blaze under your entire organization. Opportunities like this do not come along often in the life of an organization

"The art of communication is the language of leadership."
James Humes

ACTION INITIATORS

◆ At the Strategic Planning Session, share the draft vision with the planning team, carefully and methodically, paragraph by paragraph.
◆ Openly solicit reactions and responses, encouraging full disclosure of all planning team members.
◆ Encourage the planning team to make suggestions to strengthen the vision.
◆ Incorporate appropriate suggested changes immediately into the vision.
◆ Determine the core values and beliefs. Use the *Mission to Mars* exercise to help with progress.
◆ Construct the mission and purpose statement.
◆ Develop your organization's brand promise.
◆ Prior to concluding the Strategic Planning Session, finalize the updated vision with core values and beliefs, mission and purpose statement, and brand promise.
◆ Share the updated Strategic Planning Session documents with the balance of your organization's staff in a celebratory, informational event.
◆ Bring the entire organization up to speed on the strategic planning effort, and communicate what lies ahead in the process to complete the endeavor.

8

KEY PERFORMANCE ISSUES

"Realists do not fear the results of their study."

Fyodor Dostoevsky

Key performance issues are issues that are crucial to optimizing our individual or organizational performance *and* ensuring the health and longevity of our organization.

Figure 6.2 in Chapter 6 included a section of specific questions aimed at 16 critical areas within your organization that may or may not be either accelerating or inhibiting the ability to move toward your vision. These 16 identified areas are the key performance issues.

One hallmark of all the processes revolves around a pivotal central thesis: If you have great people in your business, they know your company better than anyone else. You and your staff collectively possess the insights and the know-how to precisely identify and meticulously resolve any problems that exist in your company and in your markets. This ability allows you to help overcome any and all of the identified key performance issues facing your organization. The answers to resolving these key performance issues reside in each person. The task is to tap the collective knowledge, arriving at the answer collaboratively.

"The only difference between a problem and a
solution is that most people understand the solution."

Charles F. Kettering

The information that comes to you through your internal strategic planning survey helps you locate and isolate the valuable perceptions key people embrace regarding the full spectrum of issues. Within their survey responses lay the seeds of decisive awareness and understanding.

The answer to resolving your key performance issues requires that you do three things—

1. Understand the issues clearly.
2. Create a well-designed plan to resolve the issues aggressively.
3. Set your well-conceived plan into immediate and massive motion.

As you review the survey responses during the Strategic Planning Session keep in mind that it will be the first time many of the people will lay eyes on the collection of expressed opinions and observations. This also may be the case for you. Still, pay close attention to reactions as everyone reads and reviews the solicited comments. Watch their body language.

◆ How are they reacting to what they're reading?

◆ Is it clear how people are reacting or difficult to interpret?

◆ Does the survey content leave them looking uncomfortable?

◆ Are they nodding in animated agreement as they ponder the comments of others?

◆ Are they serious in their reaction?

◆ Is the body language supportive and validating?

The reactions of the readers, collectively and individually, will provide further insights as to how you should evaluate the survey answers.

"Reality leaves a lot to the imagination."

John Lennon

CATEGORIES OF KEY PERFORMANCE ISSUES

The 16 categories that make up the key performance issues have been selected and defined to cover the full field of topics affecting an organization's ability to grow while remaining healthy and strong during the journey. The 16 categories address the spectrum of issues you will specifically want and need to tackle in your strategic plan to effectively contend with the complete range of legitimate threats, obstacles, and challenges facing the organization. The *Sweet Sixteen* key performance issues categories include:

◆ Leadership team

◆ Sales and marketing

◆ Growth

◆ Operations

◆ Market positioning and targeting

◆ Financial performance and profitability

◆ Productivity

◆ Quality and quality control

◆ Accounting information for decision making

◆ Teamwork and communication

◆ Products, services, and product/service development

◆ Training and staff development

◆ Customer satisfaction

◆ Equipment and tools

◆ Information technology and technology tools

◆ Other required resources

The content of each of these 16 key performance issues areas has not been included yet to allow each participant to formulate individual thoughts and responses. By leaving these 16 areas undefined, each respondent operates from a wide-open and uninhibited point of reference. By not reining in and narrowing their orientation and answers in each category, you encourage a freer, more open flow of perspectives, observations, ideas, and contributions.

"There is a time in the life of every problem when it is big enough to see, yet small enough to solve."

Mike Leavitt

The key performance issue are defined after the surveys are completed.

Leadership Team—Issues that affect, or are affected by, the ownership, leadership, and top management levels of the organization. Often they are referred to as the executive team as the leadership team. What are they doing or not doing to be more effective and responsive to the needs of the organization, to the people in it, and to the markets they serve?

Sales and Marketing—What are the issues affecting the top line of the organization? What are we doing or not doing that causes us to fall short of our revenue-producing potential?

Growth—Our vision calls for us to increase our business at a certain rate of growth. What are we not doing or should we not be doing to attain the desired and optimal growth rate required to turn our vision into reality?

Operations—What are we not doing or should we be doing in terms of operational practices, processes, rhythms, and rituals to smooth out our flow of business, reducing friction and stress within our organization, making it easier to do business with customers and among ourselves?

Market Positioning and Targeting—What have we not done or should we not do to successfully position our organization, to fully and properly capitalize on our desired base of identified customers and markets?

Financial Performance and Profitability—What are the issues affecting the organization's bottom line? What are we doing or not doing that causes us to fall short of our profit-producing potential? What factors are keeping us from maintaining advantageous profit margins?

Productivity—Where is our productivity not being optimized? What are we not doing or should we not be doing to maximize efficiencies? What is keeping us from fully capitalizing on our competencies?

Quality and Quality Control—Where and how are we producing and delivering less than our expected and capable level of quality? How can we guarantee our quality assurance systems are functioning at ideal levels, within the best tolerances our technology, equipment, people, and resources allow?

Accounting Information for Decision Making—What facets or elements of our accounting, documentation, reporting, or information systems are not meeting the standards we have established for these processes and systems? Where do we have significant room, or need, for improvement?

Teamwork and Communication—Where are we falling short on meeting the organization's need, or desire, for improved internal or external teamwork and communication?

Products, Services, and Product/Service Development—What are the gaps in researching and developing innovative products and services that might help us meet both current and future market needs and gain a meaningful, competitive advantage? What is the market demanding, or requesting, that we are remiss in not addressing in terms of new products and services?

Training and Staff Development—Where are we failing to meet staff needs for training and professional skills development? What are the specific needs and what do we need to do to meet the needs throughout the organization?

Customer Satisfaction—Where are we failing, to whatever degree, in meeting the needs and expectations of our customers? Where are we jeopardizing customers or losing customers to our competitors? What are the causes of any erosion of our customer base?

Equipment and Tools—What equipment and tool needs are being ignored or minimized against the needs and requests of our people? What effects are equipment and tool shortages, or needs, having on productivity, morale, meeting delivery deadlines, customer expectations, customer relations, and profit margins?

Information Technology and Technology Tools—What information and technology tool gaps exist in our organization? How do any gaps affect our market reputation, our ability to compete, and our future competitive position?

Other Required Resources—What other resources, if any, are required to make us more competitive, strengthen the market appeal of our organization, increase our ability to drive greater revenues, attract and retain top talent, and drive greater profitability to our bottom line?

These definitions fit into our planning sequence and set up a fluid transition for awareness and knowledge, becoming a distinctive list of high-potential, actionable items in the formulation of your strategic plan.

> *"Problems are the price of progress. Don't bring me*
> *anything but trouble. Good news weakens me."*
>
> *Charles F. Kettering*

IDENTIFY KEY PERFORMANCE ISSUES

Going through the key performance issues portion of the strategic planning survey, you're looking for common themes in each category—clusters of similar or linked observations, opinions, or perceptions.

◆ Where are people offering frequent and disturbingly consistent insights?

◆ Where are there universal attitudes and beliefs emerging in the comments?

◆ What are the associations made on topics of widespread agreement?

Keep in mind that where there is a crowd forming, you often have a problem taking shape. It is important to remember the bigger and more vocal the crowd, the greater the potential magnitude of your problem. Now's your opportunity to uncover painful and costly key performance issues before they get bigger and uglier, while there's still plenty of time to take prompt, effective corrective action. Doing so right now will save you a lot of grief, a lot of time, and a lot of money.

After you identify the trends in the key performance issues, patterns will show essential strategic planning skill set.

> *"The truth of the matter is that you always know*
> *the right thing to do. The hard part is doing it."*
>
> *General Norman Schwarzkopf*

IDENTIFY OBSTACLES, BARRIERS, AND CHOKEPOINTS

One of the focal strategies in warfare is to identify a battlefield's chokepoint and take the steps necessary to attack it, overpower it, occupy it, and turn it to your advantage. Turn the chokepoint into your strongpoint. In your strategic planning process, most identified key performance issues serve as impediments and obstructions, blocking and delaying the successful march toward our vision, in varying degrees of severity.

As you evaluate key performance issues in your strategic planning survey, keep in mind that among the issues that emerge as obstacles and barriers there may likely be a few that have the potential to qualify as chokepoints. A chokepoint can be defined as pivotal issues upon which eventual success—or ultimate failure—depend for you and your organization. Chokepoints become your most urgent and highest-priority conflicts and must receive your most immediate and total level of attention. In your top 5 and first of 5 goal-setting process, it is quite literally your first of 5.

So what are the obstacles and barriers in your business today? What you discover, how you perceive it, and how you interpret your strategic planning survey will impact your selection of strategies and courses of action in the strategic planning process.

"The reality of life is that your perceptions, right or wrong, influence
everything else you do. When you get a proper perspective of your
perceptions, you may be surprised by how many other things fall into place."

Roger Birkman

ADDRESS KEY PERFORMANCE ISSUES

One of the most effective and precise ways to address the key performance issues facing you and your business is through a proven process called the Hoshin Methods. The Hoshin Methods first came to prominence in the late 1980s as part of the shift to more effective production and problem-solving processes introduced by Japanese business and industry. Edwin B. Dean, a rocket scientist at NASA, describes the application of the Hoshin Method in these terms: "It's a system for translating the organization's vision, goals, and objectives into actionable and measurable strategies throughout the company."

Learning to efficiently and effectively use the Hoshin Methods will revolutionize approaches to problem solving. There will be virtually no problem or challenge you cannot successfully address, work through, and overcome. The explanation for how the Hoshin process works has been simplified, making it both easy to understand and easy to share and execute within your own organization.

Once you've completed the initial steps in the Hoshin Solutions Session, and sorted out the common themes surrounding your top goal, you are ready to close the loop on your challenge. This gets you one step closer to completing your strategic plan. The next steps in the Hoshin Methods include those listed in the chart below.

The Hoshin Methods can accelerate your analysis and resolution of any challenge facing your organization. It can help you turn an overwhelming problem into a manageable challenge. It can align your teams around solutions that make sense, regardless of resources or circumstances.

"Your life is the sum result of all the choices you make, both consciously and
unconsciously. If you can control the process of choosing, you can take control of all
aspects of your life. You can find the freedom that comes from being in charge of yourself."

Robert F. Bennett

THE NEXT STEP: HOSHIN ACTION PLANS FOR YOUR KEY PERFORMANCE ISSUES

After completing your initial round of Hoshin solutions sessions, take your planning to new stages of sophistication and precision by using the 6-Step Hoshin action plan process. Each of the key performance issues you've uncovered will be addressed in a logical, disciplined and orderly manner, resulting in an organized set of detailed action plans. Here is how you should proceed:

FIGURE 8.1—HOSHIN METHODS

The Hoshin Methods

1. **Articulate a single question** and place it on a chart board before the solutions group. Phrase the single question in the form of the goal or outcome you seek. An example might be: "How do we get from the Earth to the Moon?"

2. **Brainstorm ideas for 5 to 10 minutes** in a solutions session.

3. Have members of the group write **each** of their ideas **on a single** post-it note.

4. At the conclusion of the solutions session ask the group to individually **assign a numerical value to each of their written ideas.** The total number of points each individual has to distribute among their ideas is 50. Have them write their weighted value for each idea in the lower right-hand corner of each post-it note.

5. On the chart board, under the articulated question, **group similar ideas** or pieces of information by physically moving the notes **bearing similar themes** together. Eliminate any redundant ideas from multiple notes.

6. Establish a "header" or title for each group of common ideas or themes.

7. Write each "header" or title as a "verb-noun" phrase. For example: "Conduct Awareness Training."

8. If there are too many notes in any single grouping, create another sub-grouping by identifying a finer distinction than the original heading. Set aside any "loner" or single note ideas and give them their own heading, if appropriate. Otherwise, sideline them for later consideration.

9. Add up the values recorded on each note within a grouping and record the grouping total on the header. Ideas with higher scores are perceived to be those with higher potential impact.

Outcome: A set of relationships, grouped by common themes, weighted by perceived or potential impact and value.

FIGURE 8.2—HOSHIN METHODS

The Hoshin Methods

what to do next to successfully finish the Hoshin problem solutions session:

1. Determine the driving elements, sequencing, and flow of the headings necessary to produce an orderly set of solutions to your single question.

2. Start with any two headings. Ask the questions "Which happens first?" and "Which influences the other?" Draw a one-way arrow to indicate the sequence or flow, from initial to secondary, and identify the direction of priority and influence.

3. If there is a two-way or simultaneous relationship between the headers, determine which of the headers is more dominant and direct the arrow accordingly.

4. Ask the questions "Which happens first?" and "Which influences the other?" for all of the headers on the chart board, determining the relationships of priority and influence for all header entries. Draw all the appropriate arrows until *all* header relationships are defined.

5. Count the number of arrows going TOWARD each header and record that number in the upper right-hand corner of each header.

6. The scores for the headers will determine the sequencing of your solution, in descending order, from the lowest score to the highest score. That is, you will likely begin solving your issue, sequentially, at the header with a score of "0," progressing through headers with scores of "1," "2," "3," and so on until all headers are covered. This is your solutions flow.

7. Headers with lower scores are considered drivers: higher urgency and priority.

Outcome: A detailed map of the cause and effect relationships, potential solutions, and sequence flow to your key performance issues or problem, including the key drivers that will allow you to leverage and direct your efforts *and* expedite the implementation of effective solutions.

CREATING HOSHIN ACTION PLANS

6-STEP FOLLOW-UP AND COMPLETION PROCEDURES

To create and complete the Hoshin action plans for each of the key performance issues, follow these six sequential steps:

1. Assign key performance issues (KPI) areas leaders convene a group to complete the Hoshin analysis for each of their assigned KPI categories. Each group consists of two to five individuals, individuals with either a vested interest in the issue itself or specific expertise in the KPI area.
2. During the Hoshin analysis meeting, the group sorts through all of the headers/themes, the flow and sequence of actions from each header/theme, and the Hoshin post-it solutions from the Strategic Planning Session Hoshin processes. The group determines the sequence and priority of each proposed solution or action. At the direction and discretion of the KPI area leader, the group also determines which proposed solutions or actions are doable in terms of timing, resources, and impact and which are not doable.

   Nonused solutions or actions should NOT be discarded. Instead, they should be side-lined for future consideration.
3. After the highest-potential solutions and actions have been defined, they are entered on the "Hoshin Action Plan Template." When filled in properly, the plan will look something like the chart below.
4. After you've finished defining the actions/solutions and finished tentatively plugging in the "who" and the "by when" each action will be completed, go deeper under each action/solution and define the more specific, numerous, and appropriate action steps required to produce the desired results by the targeted due date(s). An example of a properly finished output might look something like the chart below.
5. Complete this process for all headers/themes within the KPI area assigned to each leader. When this full analysis is completed for every header/theme, turn in your KPI action plans documentation to the person in your organization assigned to collect the finished strategic plan materials. This person should then forward the compiled and collected action plan materials to the assigned strategic plan editor who will be in charge of incorporating the work output into the finished strategic plan for your organization.
6. The KPI area leaders should *begin implementing their assigned KPI action plans immediately,* using the new plans to monitor actions, accountabilities, and deadlines.

By following these six steps you will gain an immediate and aggressive advantage as you begin pursuing your vision and strategic plan. Following these six steps closely provides clarity and confidence for your team of planners, as you face the task of formalizing action plans.

> *"Understand that most problems are a good sign. Problems indicate that progress is being made, wheels are turning, and you are moving towards your goals. Beware when you believe you have no problems, because then you've really got a problem!"*
>
> *Scott Alexander*

ASSIGN KEY PERFORMANCE ISSUES

After you've completed the Hoshin action plans for your organization as directed above, you will need to capture all of the output in narrative form and include the narrative action plans in your strategic plan.

FIGURE 8.3—HOSHIN ACTION PLANS

The Hoshin Process

Key Performance Issues Action Plan

Key Performance Issues Area: Market Needs/Targeting/Positioning

Area Owner(s): Robert Maister

Key Performance Issues Question: How do we ensure we're providing products that potential buyers will willingly purchase at full market prices?

Header/Theme: Analyze, Monitor, and Adjust our Product Line.	Who	When
1. Provide products that best fit targeted buyers' profiles.	RM	9/15
2. Show greater flexibility in making adjustments to buyer requests.	RM	8/1
3. Provide products with a greater range of versatile options.	JB	8/31
4. Improve the quality of our product offerings.	JW	8/15
5. Continually update our product's features.	KT	8/31
6. Create a more enjoyable buying experience for our customers.	CG	8/1
7. Provide products that are appealing to a broader range of lifestyles.	RM	9/30
8. Monitor and manage product quality to maintain superior levels.	JW	8/7
9. Seek greater creativity in new product features.	RS	8/24
10. Reduce time required to add new features to product production cycle.	GH	8/21

FIGURE 8.4—HOSHIN ACTION PLANS

The Hoshin Process

Key Performance Issues Action Plan

Key Performance Issues Area: Market Needs/Targeting/Positioning

Area Owner(s): Robert Maister

Key Performance Issues Question: How do we ensure we're providing products that potential buyers will willingly purchase at full market prices?

Header/Theme: Analyze, Monitor, and Adjust our Product Line.	Who	When
1. Provide products that best fit targeted buyer profiles.	RM	9/15
a. Review existing buyer profiles to better understand needs.	KE	8/5
b. Compare profiles and needs to our existing product lines.	SR	8/10
c. Determine appropriate adjustments to our product lines.	RM	8/21
d. Incorporate adjustments into our product production processes.	PA	9/7
2. Show greater flexibility in making adjustments to buyer requests.	RM	8/1

ACTION INITIATORS

◆ During the Strategic Planning Session, review internal strategic planning surveys, identifying the key performance issues contained in the compiled responses.
◆ Pinpoint obstacles, barriers, and chokepoints in the survey feedback.
◆ Conduct Hoshin breakout sessions during the Strategic Planning Session.
◆ Use the Hoshin methods for addressing and resolving your key performance issues obstacles, barriers, and chokepoints.
◆ Create detailed Hoshin action plans for all the themes identified in your Hoshin breakout sessions.
◆ Assign Hoshin action plan accountabilities and due dates for all documented actions.
◆ Begin implementing and executing the Hoshin action plans immediately, without delay.

9

THE WRITING PLAN

"The secret of getting ahead is getting started."

Sally Berger

The strategic plan consists of 15 sections. The 15 assignable sections are called the operational strategic plan (outlined in Table 1.1 in Chapter 1). The sections include:

1. Cover page, title page, nondisclosure agreement, and table of contents
2. The executive summary
3. Company direction statement
4. Vision, mission/purpose, core values, and brand promise
5. Company overview
6. Product and service strategies
7. Market analysis
8. Sales and marketing plan
9. Operations plan
10. Information technology plan
11. Financial plan overview
12. Issues, goals, and action plans
13. Staffing plan
14. Full financial plan data
15. Supporting data exhibits, if required

These 15 sections will be further explained in Chapter 10. Before addressing the specifics of *what* will be in your plan, there are issues to address and decisions to make.

"The difference between failure and success is doing a thing nearly right and doing it exactly right."

Edward Simmons

PLAN EDITOR

The first step to take is to decide who will preside over the entire strategic plan writing and development project. This person will be the plan editor. This important role is optimally assigned to a person with a honed set of writing skills, superb leadership talent, proven organization abilities, a sense of adventure, and the unreserved desire to direct the project. This imperative leadership role represents a noteworthy opportunity for someone with the aspirations to guide a project with major impact on the organization's future. It is no small undertaking, nor is it an assignment to be taken lightly. The role and responsibilities of the plan editor are to insist upon everyone's best creative and productive efforts throughout the project's duration, to coordinate and direct the overall inventive adventure, and to assure that everyone hits production deadlines.

Among the first questions to answer are these—

1. Who among us is *most qualified* to fill this important role?
2. Who among us is *most interested* in filling this important role?
3. Who among us is *most available* to fill this role?
4. Given the demands of the role and the realities of our business over the next 8 to 10 weeks, who is our *first and best choice* to lead this project?

The actual authoring and writing responsibilities for each section of the plan should be allocated and assigned to the appropriate person possessing the following abilities:

1. The ability to lead and manage the specific areas covered in each section.
2. The expertise required to think and problem solve creatively and write authoritatively on the subjects comprising the section.
3. The required writing skills to competently capture and communicate effectively the content and detail of the section.

In other words, choose and assign the writing assignments to those who know the most, care the most, can think and execute most strategically, and can put their best efforts into the all-inclusive writing effort of each plan section.

These assignments are extremely important to the success of your overall strategic planning effort. The people you select to fill the roles of section authors need to be fully committed to the value and execution of their assignments. Among the questions to ask, before you select the most appropriate authors for each section, are these—

1. Who is *most qualified* to lead the writing of this section?
2. Who is *most interested* in filling this important role?
3. Who may be *the most appropriate* person to fill the role of writing this section?
4. Who among us is *most available* to fill this role so that we can meet our plan production deadlines?
5. Given the demands of the role and the realities of our business over the next 8 to 10 weeks, who is our *first and best choice* to lead the creation and completion of this section?

Using the qualifying questions listed above, narrow the field of appropriate candidates for each section author.

SECTION EDITORS

The accountability for writing each of the plan sections requires assigned authors to pace their labors and meet all interim production deadlines. Each assigned section author is responsible for guiding the creation of the section's content and for organizing and leading the significant amount of thought and problem solving involved that are important components. The section authors determine who they want and need to join them in the process of researching and evaluating the data, insights, and conclusions that fall within their sectional domains and mandates. The assigned section authors are the primary coordinators of each section writing team's effort and eventual output.

> *"Every action we take, everything we do, is either a victory or a defeat in the struggle to become what we want to be."*
>
> *Anne Byrhhe*

DUE DATES

When you launch the writing of the Strategic Business Plan, you should set a target completion date for the first drafts of each plan section at 8 to 10 weeks from the point that Strategic Planning Sessions are tangibly completed. This time frame generally allows each of the section authors enough time for research and sufficient time to consider impacts of their strategies, tactics, and eventually recommended courses of action. This also allows abundant time to bounce their preliminary discoveries and proposals off of other planning team members.

> *"Indecision and delays are the parents of failure."*
>
> *George Canning*

ACQUIRE AND ENCOURAGE THE DISCIPLINE OF WRITING AND FINISHING THE PLAN

The most difficult aspect of writing the plan can be gaining and exercising the required level of discipline. A hefty measure of self-regulation is required for sustaining a regimented rhythm and a productive intensity.

The first few hours will be invested in research and in collecting the knowledge to organize thoughts, draw conclusions, formulate strategies, and develop tactics and plans of action. Writing usually occurs about three weeks into the process. It is at this customary point that the pace of actual production quickens and a draft begins to emerge.

The length of each section averages somewhere between 6 and 15 pages, with a more customary average of about 8 to 10 pages per section for most organizations. With these parameters in mind, set a modest goal of finishing two to three draft pages per week, during the 8 to 10 weeks before the section draft is due. This type of pacing allows you to invest ample time and attention in pressing forward with your strategic planning duties, without sacrificing any degree of attentiveness to the regular daily and weekly organizational duties.

The last consideration for you and other members of your section team is collaboration. Share your output for input: Solicit and encourage no-holds-barred feedback. Allow others to review and critique your writing as the section draft evolves. Be fearless in seeking critical comment, reaction, and advice. And when you do obtain it, avoid being defensive. The input you receive will strengthen the plan and lead to the production of a powerful finished draft.

> *"In many lines of work it isn't how much you do that counts,*
> *but how much you do well and how often you decide right."*
>
> *William Feather*

ACTION INITIATORS

- Select a plan editor. This person is responsible for presiding over the entire Strategic Business Plan writing process.
- Assign plan writing responsibilities for each section of the plan. Allocate a fair share to every qualified person on the Strategic Planning Team.
- To ensure that the plan writing workload is spread equitably, no single person should have responsibility for writing more than four sections.
- Set a completion date for the production and delivery of all written plan section drafts. Generally, production periods run 8 to 10 weeks.
- Section authors should convene meetings with their selected section teams to assign interim due dates for team production.
- Establish and faithfully adhere to daily disciplines and daily rhythms of production.
- Collaborate and solicit interim feedback on your assigned section output from others, both inside and outside of your plan section writing team. Incorporate applicable suggestions into your evolving plan section drafts.

After the plan writing process commences, meet all plan writing deadlines and due dates.

SECTION III
IMPLEMENTATION

10

DRAFT THE PLAN

"Writing crystallizes thought, and thought produces action."

Paul J. Meyer

The most daunting part of beginning the actual writing of the Strategic Business Plan is figuring out both *how* and *where* to start. So many major questions, and so few definitive answers, exist at this early stage of the creative process.

First, build an outline of the thoughts, concepts, and ideas you want to communicate. Lay out the initial outline of the broad topics you want to cover. Then fill in your expanding outline to make your intentions ever clearer, magnifying the clarity with each additional idea.

To make this process even easier, follow a clear path of proper questions. These questions will help create and develop your plan narrative. EMT has generated a comprehensive, time-tested series of questions drawn from among a multitude of resources.

The questions have been refined and upgraded to the full set of strategic plan question prompts. These prompts will make your Strategic Business Plan writing assignment as simple and manageable as possible. By simply addressing the clear path questions that follow this chapter, you'll find your progress accelerating to complete your strategic plan.

THE EXECUTIVE SUMMARY

The purpose of the executive summary is to provide a detailed snapshot of the entire Strategic Business Plan for any interested reader. The executive summary delivers the prominent, leading, and most significant elements of the plan in an easily digestible portion. More than any other section of the plan, this one will attract the most readers. Upon viewing the executive summary, any reader should be left with the opinion that the company has a clearly defined direction, well-conceived and accurate strategies, and manageable actions to drive the organization reliably towards its vision. The clear path executive summary questions you need to answer are listed below.

BACKGROUND AND CURRENT SITUATION

How many employees are in your organization at this time?
In general terms, what are their roles?
Describe in detail your current facilities.
Describe the industry that you're in and the current state of your industry.
Describe the current state or standing of your organization within your industry.

CORPORATE INFORMATION

What is the legal form of your organization?
Where are you headquartered?

Do you have any other offices or facilities? If so, provide details.

FINANCIAL PERFORMANCE AND FORECASTS

Provide a narrative of financial performance since the founding of your organization. Detail trends, highs, lows, consistency of performance, and present versus historical performance.

Provide a narrative of your company's financial performance over the last three years. Detail trends, consistency of performance, and present versus historical performance.

Provide a narrative synopsis of the over-arching strategies envisioned to guide and grow the organization, along with all the supportive strategies developed in your Strategic Planning Session.

Provide a narrative highlight of plan forecasted financial performance, as you anticipate it will unfold, over the next three to five years for your organization, aligning with your strategies and plans for growth and healthy performance.

PERFORMANCE OBJECTIVES

List the top 5 and first of 5 long-term goals for the organization for the next 5 to 10 years.
List the top 5 and first of 5 intermediate-term goals for the organization for the next 2 to 3 years.
List the top 5 and first of 5 short-term goals for the organization for the next 12 months.

CAPITAL REQUIREMENTS

What are the anticipated capital requirements for the organization, to fund the growth plan, if any?
How, specifically, will the funds/capital be used?

MANAGEMENT TEAM

List all of the owners, officers, shareholders, and key managers in the organization, along with titles, if any, and years of experience within their roles or within your industry.

List the names, organizations, and respective roles of your principal advisors: attorney(s), accountant(s), business advisors and consultant(s), and the like.

Provide an abbreviated overview of the exit strategies and succession plans for any envisioned transitions in ownership or leadership anticipated for the organization during the period covered by the plan.

SALES STRATEGY

Describe your organization's sales objectives.
Describe your organization's sales plan and strategies, as they exist today and as they address the performance forecasts for this plan.
Who are your present customers or clients? Provide a comprehensive listing.
Who are your highest-priority prospects? Provide a comprehensive listing.
Who are your intermediate-priority prospects? Provide a comprehensive listing.
Describe in overview your sales staffing at present.
Describe in overview your sales training and sales development processes at present.

SERVICE STRATEGIES

Describe in detail the products and services offered by your organization.
Describe in overview new products or services your organization intends to bring to the market over the coming one to five years and include sufficient detail to outline introduction strategies for each.

MARKET ANALYSIS

What are the trends presently emerging in your market?
What is the upside of present market trends?
What is the downside of present market trends?
Describe in overview your customer profile.
Describe in overview your top customers at this time. Who are they? How long have they been customers?
  What percentage of total annual sales volume does each represent? Highlight opportunities to expand sales volume with each customer.

COMPETITION

Who are your top five competitors?
Individually, assess the strengths, weaknesses, and vulnerabilities of your top five competitors as they exist today.
What are the competitive threats to your organization, as they exist today?
Do you see those competitive threats changing in the next 12 to 36 months? If so, how will they change?
What are the competitive opportunities facing your organization today? Please detail.

RISKS

What are the top business risks facing your organization today?
What are the top economic risks facing your organization today?

MARKETING PLAN

Describe in overview your organization's overall strategic marketing objectives.
Describe in overview your organization's overall marketing plan, as it exists today.
Describe in overview your organization's advertising and promotion plan, as it exists today.
Describe in overview your organization's public relations and publicity plan, as it exists today.

> *"The most essential gift for a good writer is a built-in, shock-proof bullshit protector. This is the writer's radar, and all the great writers have it."*
>
> *Ernest Hemingway*

COMPANY DIRECTION

The company direction section is designed to provide greater detail on two levels: Where is the organization today? Where is the organization headed as it moves into the future? This section deals with the strategic nuts and bolts of the organization. It asks you to clarify for your reader where you see yourself at this moment and identify precisely where you intend to go from here, in expansive layers of detail.

The clear path company direction questions facing you include:

Describe in detail your organization's current business. What does your business do?
Describe, in detail, the organization's history.

STRATEGIES FOR MAINTAINING AND GROWING THE BUSINESS

What are your philosophies regarding clients and customers?
How do you attract new customers/clients?

Specifically, what are the strategies you will pursue and the actions you will take to attract new customers/clients?

How do you intend to retain customers/clients, strategically?

Specifically, what are the actions you will take to retain customers/clients?

What do your customers/clients say about your organization and how it conducts business?

MANAGEMENT AND STAFFING

Is your entire management and leadership team in place? If so, detail the makeup of your existing management and leadership team.

If not, what specific actions will you take to bring your leadership and management team to full strength and effectiveness?

Are all of your leadership and management team members "keepers"? If not, please describe.

Are there any changes due to take place in the next 12 months with your management and leadership team lineup? If so, detail.

Is a succession/transition plan in place for leadership? If so, please describe.

How many people are included in the organization's top leadership positions? Who are they? What are their positions? How long have they been with the organization? What are their specific roles and responsibilities?

What is the expected growth in staff levels over the next 12 months?

What is the average tenure of existing staff members, in years of service?

What is current staff turnover on an annual basis? Is it higher or lower than industry averages? What is the trend against historical averages for your organization?

"You must get involved to have an impact. No one is impressed with the won-lost record of the referee."

John H. Holcomb

FACILITIES

Describe in detail your present facilities and office space: Square footage? Location? Address? Occupied for how long?

What are the terms of your present lease? When does the lease come up for renewal? What is the cost per square foot on an annual basis through expiration of the present lease term?

Who is your landlord? Provide full contact data on your landlord. Describe the quality of the relationship you have with your landlord presently.

Do you have plans for a move in the next one to five years? If so, please detail.

PRODUCTS AND SERVICES

What products or services do you provide? Please describe each primary product or service in detail.

MARKET ENVIRONMENT

Describe in detail your present industry, market, and market trends.

CLIENTS AND CUSTOMERS

Describe the qualities that make up clients and customers in your present base of business.

Describe the "ideal" customer for your organization. What is their profile?

Why do present customers and clients choose to do business with your organization?

PRICING AND PROFITABILITY

Describe your organization's history of profitability.

Describe the present environment for profitable performance in your industry and in your business.

Describe your organization's orientation to future levels of profitability.

Specifically, what are the strategies and actions you will execute to increase future profitability?

Can you be profitable at present industry pricing levels? If so, describe your strategies and plans to optimize profitability. If not, please describe the present situation and its impact on your thinking in your present plan.

Describe your organization's present cash flow situation.

Specifically, what are the strategies you will employ and actions you will take to improve future cash flow?

FINANCIAL STATUS AND CRITICAL PERFORMANCE NUMBERS

What are the key/critical performance numbers you presently monitor?

What are the key/critical performance numbers you will add and/or monitor in the future? What are your new goal performance benchmarks, to improve operational productivity and enhance overall profitability and financial performance?

COMPANY OVERVIEW

The company overview section is designed to provide greater detail on the operational nuts and bolts of the organization. For this section you will gather, compile, and clarify for your reader information on the legal, regulatory, geographical, and advisory details of the business. For many organizations, few people have all of the details in this section of the plan at their fingertips. By building this section of the strategic plan you bring all of the essential elements together in one unified place, for the benefit of the entire management team, the board of directors, or any prospective investors or shareholders. The basis for having all of these materials and this knowledge in one place—in the strategic plan—is to ensure a single, centralized repository of this data and knowledge should the need to peruse it arise.

The clear path company overview questions for you to address are:

What is the full legal name of the organization?

Are there any subsidiary organizations tied directly or indirectly to this organization? If so, describe in detail.

LEGAL FORM OF BUSINESS OR ORGANIZATION

Describe the legal form of the organization. "C" corporation? "S" corporation? Partnership? LLC? Other? Full details, please.

BUSINESS LOCATION

What is the location of the primary offices and facilities of the organization?

What are the locations of other offices or facilities in the organization, if any?

GOVERNMENT REGULATIONS AFFECTING ORGANIZATION

Describe the regulatory agencies, if any, that have jurisdiction over you and your organization. Describe the quality of the relationship you presently have with each regulatory agency.

In what state(s) is your organization licensed to conduct business?

Describe in detail the license(s), permit(s), or certification(s), if any, under which you operate.

Is your organization presently operating under any legal, financial, or regulatory restrictions in the conduct of its business? If so, please detail.

What certifications or professional qualifications are held by your organization or its staff members to establish credibility and credentials for performance capabilities?

To what industry trade groups or professional associations does your organization affiliate, participate, or support? To what extent are you involved with each group or association?

OUTSIDE SUPPORT: LEGAL, ACCOUNTING, AND ADVISORY SERVICE RESOURCES

Please provide the details of these important relationships for your organization.

PRIMARY BUSINESS ADVISOR

Name:
Firm:
Education:
Background business biography:
Primary services provided:
Primary contributions to success of your organization:

SECONDARY BUSINESS ADVISOR

Name:
Firm:
Education:
Background business biography:
Primary services provided:
Primary contributions to success of your organization:

PRIMARY LEGAL ADVISOR

Name:
Firm:
Education:
Background business biography:
Primary services provided:
Primary contributions to success of your organization:

SECONDARY LEGAL ADVISOR (IF APPLICABLE)

Name:
Firm:
Education:
Background business biography:
Primary services provided:
Primary contributions to success of your organization:

PRIMARY ACCOUNTING ADVISOR

Name:
Firm:
Education:
Background business biography:
Primary services provided:
Primary contributions to success of your organization:

OTHER ADVISOR (IF APPLICABLE)

Name:
Firm:
Education:
Background business biography:
Primary services provided:
Primary contributions to success of your organization:

> *"The road to success is always under construction."*
>
> *Jim Miller*

THE LEADERSHIP TEAM AND STAFFING PLAN

The clear path leadership team and staffing plan questions consist of:

MANAGEMENT AND LEADERSHIP TEAM

Describe your management and leadership team: names, genders, years of combined experience, and years of individual experience.

OFFICERS AND KEY EMPLOYEES

Detail all names, position/roles, ages, and stock ownership percentages.
Tell us about your organization's founder(s).
Is there a stock option plan for the organization? If so, describe in detail.
Has management or ownership made any commitments for stock ownership for anyone not now a shareholder? If so, please describe the commitments.
Are there any shareholders outside the present core management team? If so, provide details.

STOCK ALLOCATION

How many shares in the organization have been authorized?
How many shares in the organization have been issued?
What is the detailed breakdown on stock allocations to date?
What is the detailed breakdown on any stock options or warrants, if any, that exist today?

MANAGEMENT RESPONSIBILITIES FOR EACH POSITION

Name:
Education:
Background business biography:
Position primary job responsibilities:
Position primary performance goals:

STAFFING

Describe your present staffing situation. Staffed correctly? Too many? Too few? Describe in detail.
Describe your strategies and actions for bringing staffing levels to required levels in all departments.

Describe your immediate staffing needs for the next 1 to 6 months.
Describe your staffing needs for the next 6 to 12 months.
Describe your staffing needs for the next 12 to 24 months.
Describe your staffing needs for the next 24 to 36 months.

STAFFING AND RECRUITING PLAN

Describe the staffing and recruiting philosophies of your organization. How do you approach attracting, recruiting, and retaining high-quality employees?
Describe the current hiring climate within your industry.
Describe the current hiring climate within your geographic region.
Is turnover within your organization within acceptable limits for your industry?
What is the turnover rate for your organization at present? How does this compare with turnover rates within your industry? Within your region?
Describe your intended strategies and actions to optimize staffing and recruiting performance as part of your plan.

STAFF DEVELOPMENT PLAN

Describe your plans to fully develop the leadership, management, and technical skills and capabilities of your staff in their range of roles and areas of responsibility within your organization.
Describe present training and development programs in use in your organization. How are they effective? What is the evidence of their effectiveness?
Describe future changes and improvements to the training and development programs intended in your organization. How will they be more effective? What is the plan to optimize their effectiveness?
Describe how you are presently assessing, developing, or planning to develop leaders and managers to fuel the growth of your organization in the coming 12 to 36 months covered by this strategic plan.

"Good writing is clear thinking made visible."

Bill Wheeler

THE SALES AND REVENUE GROWTH PLAN

The sales and revenue growth plan serves to outline and capture the details of how the organization's sales team will deliver the necessary top-line revenues to meet the sales and revenue forecasts. It is also designed to provide insights into product and service strategies that will propel sales performance.

The clear path sales and revenue growth plan questions consist of these:

Detail the full range of current products and services offered by your organization.
Detail the benefits, potential returns on investment, and/or market appeal of your current products and/or services.
Detail what you believe are your current competitive advantages in the products and/or services you offer in the market.
Detail the full range of future products and services under consideration or under development that your organization anticipates introducing over the next one to five years.
What are the timeframes for development and delivery of these future products and services by your organization?
Detail the benefits, potential returns on investment, and/or market appeal of your intended future products and/or services.

Detail what you believe are your current competitive advantages offered by the future products and/or services you intend to offer in the market.

List and detail any proprietary technologies, products, or services your organization offers or intends to offer to your clients or customers.

> *"The secret to success is to start from scratch and keep on scratching."*
>
> *Dennis Green*

RESEARCH AND DEVELOPMENT

Describe your research and development plan for new products and services or proprietary new technologies you intend to bring to market or use internally to expand the appeal or efficiencies of your organization in the market.

Describe in detail your sales strategies for increasing top-line revenues.

Do you have a formal sales plan that allocates sales responsibilities to different individuals, either by specialty, by geographic area, by industry, by customer allocation, or the like? If so, or if not, describe in detail.

Describe your sales staffing plan. What is it currently? What will it look like as you grow your organization?

Current sales staffing plan:

    Sales staffing plan over the next 1 to 3 years

    Sales staffing plan over the next 3 to 5 or 10 years

Describe your sales compensation and benefits program or plan. How will it be used to attract and retain top sales talent, both now and in the future?

Describe your sales staff development plan for your organization.

Describe your plan for new client/new customer development.

What are the top 10, or top 25, or top 50 new client/new customer prospects for your organization to pursue and add to your client base over the next 12 to 24 months? Use the following format:

    Prospect company:

    Located in:

    Contact phone number:

    Initial contact should be with:

    Contact/qualify prospect by what date:

THE MARKETING PLAN

The marketing plan is the assembly of a multitude of elements, addressing an analysis of the following:

◆ Market and industry in which the organization competes

◆ Competition itself

◆ Market segmentation

◆ Market opportunities

◆ Branding

◆ Positioning

◆ Market mix decisions

◆ Advertising

- Marketing

- Publicity

- Public relations strategies and action plans

- Key customer acquisition and retention strategies

- Reputation enhancement plans

This section is intended to encompass an examination of the organization's current and all future markets for the company's products and services. It might well include any primary market research completed by the organization that assists in defining the market, targeted customer profiles, competitive positions, company strengths and weaknesses, and the strengths, weaknesses, and vulnerabilities of prime competitors.

The clear path marketing plan questions for you to answer are comprised of these—

Provide a thorough, current analysis of your industry, as it exists today.

Provide a comprehensive forecast of your industry and market segment as you see it evolving and changing over the next one to five years, to the best of your abilities.

Analyze your organization's place and position within your industry and your market, in both the present and the future.

Describe the specific, specialized market segment, if any, that you believe your organization presently embraces or will embrace in the future.

Describe specifically how you plan to successfully penetrate and service your targeted market or market segment.

Specifically, what are the actions you will take to increase market share?

Describe your intended strategies and actions to optimize marketing performance as you execute and implement

ANALYZE YOUR ORGANIZATION

Strengths: What gives your organization unique capabilities and capacities?
Weaknesses: What works against your best interests, your reputation, and optimal performance?
Opportunities: What exciting events or opportunities might your organization pursue?
Threats: What might keep you from attaining your vision or goals as an organization?
Barriers: What obstacles or impediments must your organization address and overcome to succeed?
Key performance issues: What are the issues you MUST resolve to maintain positive momentum?

CUSTOMER PROFILE

Describe, in detail, the profile of your average customer or client *and* the profile of your optimal customer or client.
Average customer profile:
Optimal customer profile:
Provide a full customer list current as of:

COMPETITION

List the top 5 to 10 competitors for your organization.
Individually, detail the profiles of your top 5 to 10 competitors as follows:

COMPETITOR

Name:

- Strengths: What are the unique strengths that make this competitor formidable?

◆ Weaknesses: Where is this competitor at a disadvantage?

◆ Threats: What dangerous and intimidating potential does this competitor pose?

◆ Vulnerabilities: At what points can our efforts exploit areas where this competitor is at risk?

◆ Key customers we should pursue: Which customers of this competitor should we deliberately, actively, and aggressively target?

◆ A list of all other competitors within your industry or market would include which other organizations?

OVERALL COMPETITIVE PICTURE

Combined competitor strengths:
Combined competitor weaknesses:
Combined competitor vulnerabilities:
Combined competitor threats:
Combined competitor opportunities:

COMPETITIVE STRATEGIES

To increase the overall competitiveness of your organization, what specifically must you do? Detail the specific strategies and actions you plan to take:
Immediately:
This quarter:
This fiscal year:
In the next one to t here years:

RISKS TO YOUR ORGANIZATION

What are the risks facing your organization today, in terms of:

BUSINESS RISKS

Cost and profitability structure:
Competition:
Industry growth rate:
Demand for products and services:
Client/customer loss:
Labor/talent availability:
Management succession and continuity:
Management and leadership effectiveness:
Profit margin erosion:
Professional or business liability:
Other(s):

ENVIRONMENTAL RISKS

Economic risk:
Weather and other catastrophes:

Legal and government regulatory impact:

Other(s):

Advertising, promotion, publicity, and public relations:

Describe your strategies and action plan for advertising and promoting your organization over the next 12 to 36 months. Be specific as to actions you will take.

Describe your strategies and action plan for public relations and publicity for your organization over the next 12 to 36 months. Be specific about actions you will take.

> *"Reduce your plan to writing. The moment you complete this, you will have definitely given concrete form to the intangible desire."*
>
> *Napoleon Hill*

CUSTOMER SERVICE STRATEGIES

The customer service strategies section explains how you will acquire, retain, and grow customers for your organization. They are the strategies and actions you will deploy to ensure that every customer's needs are understood, that those needs are addressed, and that the relationships with each and every one of your valued customers are nurtured to a level notably superior to which those same relationships are being pursued and nurtured by your competitors.

The clear path customer service strategies questions to concentrate your creative energies on are these:

Describe your organization's customer service vision.

Specify the measurable standards you will establish to manage and optimize customer service in your organization.

Detail the strategies and actions you will set in motion to move your organization toward your customer service vision.

> *"Take time to deliberate; but when the time for action arrives, stop thinking and go in."*
>
> *Andrew Jackson*

THE INFORMATION TECHNOLOGY PLAN

The information technology plan section is intended to express the details of your overall technology application philosophies and practices. It should also allow you to capture and communicate your expectations for any and all of those future technology applications that you expect will allow you to sustain a competitive edge while maintaining a manageable and justifiable level of investment in technology.

The clear path information technology questions that need to be thoroughly and thoughtfully considered are these:

CURRENT TECHNOLOGIES (AN OVERVIEW OF YOUR PRESENT TECHNOLOGY BASE)

What technologies do you presently have in place to assist the smooth, efficient operational functioning of your organization?

What capacities does your present technology afford?

What capabilities does your present technology offer?

What competitive advantages do you presently enjoy, if any, with your present technologies?

What weaknesses or vulnerabilities are inherent in your present technologies? What impact do they have on your organization's competitive position?

FUTURE TECHNOLOGIES

Provide a forecast of future technologies your organization must acquire, deploy, and/or refine to remain on the leading technological competitive edge of your industry as you grow in the next one to five years.

What competitive advantages will acquisition and deployment of these future technologies have for your organization?

What are the timelines and anticipated costs associated with the acquisition, installation, and operational implementation of these future technologies?

> *"The art of writing is the art of applying the seat of the pants to the seat of the chair."*
>
> *Mary Heaton Vorse*

THE OPERATIONS PLAN

The section encompassing the operations plan clarifies the specific strategies and actions your organization intends to utilize to reach optimum, sustained levels of operational efficiency and managed profitability. Properly conceived and communicated, the operations plan explains the full extent of human and operational resources required to effectively and efficiently support the sales, service, and distribution of the organization's full range of products and services. It should also define and distinguishes the strategic expectations and the supportive actions required to achieve the organization's strategic plan objectives.

The clear path operations plan questions are these:

Describe your present situation and philosophies in operations staffing.

Provide an overview of your present operations staffing: How many people? What are their roles and responsibilities?

Describe how you see operations staffing changing as you grow your organization: Numbers of people? New positions? New roles and responsibilities?

Describe/forecast annual growth levels and hiring needs for the coming five years, by individual year.

Describe the profile of a person you'd seek to fill operational vacancies within your company. What qualities are essential?

OPERATIONS STAFF COMPENSATION PLAN

Describe the compensation programs and packages currently used to compensate and motivate the entire range of operations positions in your organization.

Describe the improvements to operations compensation programs and packages that you believe will be necessary, in the future, to attract and retain top talent for your organization to fuel future growth.

OPERATIONS INFRASTRUCTURES AND CAPACITIES

Describe the full range of operations departments within your organization.

Describe the roles and structure of each of the departments that make up your organization's operations. Describe in terms of roles, goals, accountabilities, processes, and procedures.

Describe the strengths of your present operations departments and your operations staff.

Describe the capabilities of your present operations departments and your operations staff.

Describe the competitive advantages offered by your present operations departments and staff.

Describe the weaknesses of your present operations departments and staff.

What specific actions need to be taken to strengthen operations performance over the next 12 months?

What specific actions need to be taken to strengthen operations performance over the next 12 to 24 months?

"The secret of discipline is motivation. When a man is sufficiently motivated, discipline will take care of itself."

Sir Alexander Paterson

THE FINANCIAL PLAN OVERVIEW

The financial plan overview is intended to briefly capture the distilled details of the entire financial plan. This section follows the strategic plan. After the executive summary, it is the second most-read section of the strategic plan. For strictly bottom-line readers, in fact, this is often the first section they seek. This section should also contain a recap of the organization's critical numbers and the desired operating financial ratios, which serve as the internal benchmarks for comprehending, monitoring, and managing the overall fiscal performance of the business.

The clear path financial plan overview questions you will want to account for include:

FINANCIAL FORECASTS AND BUDGETS

What are the full range of assumptions on which your full financial plan are based?

FINANCIAL STATEMENTS OVERVIEW

Year	Year 1	Year 2	Year 3	Year 4	Year 5
Total Revenues					
% Growth					
$ Growth					
Net Income Before Tax					
Net Profit %					

CAPITAL REQUIREMENTS

What are the capital requirements for your business, if any, as covered in your plan over the next one to five years?
For what specific purposes will your capital requirements be used?

FINANCIAL PLAN CONCLUSIONS

What conclusions for this financial plan do you want drawn to the attention of any person reading this document?

"Never tell people how to do things. Tell them what to do, and they will surprise you with their ingenuity."

General George S. Patton

THE COMPREHENSIVE ORGANIZATION STAFFING PLAN

The comprehensive organization staffing plan is a graphic representation of all staffing growth, presented year-by-year in the form of three to six expanding organizational charts. The charts detail every member of the existing staff on hand at the beginning of each fiscal year, as well as show all planned additions to staff throughout the year, by both position and anticipated date of hire. This series of charts helps management foresee when is the best time to begin trying to fill forecasted staff openings.

*"What no spouse of a writer can understand is that a writer
is working when he's staring out of the window."*

Burton Rascoe

FINANCIAL FORECASTS AND BUDGETS

This section includes all financial forecasts and budgets for the periods covering the entire strategic plan. It details all financial pro forma assumptions. It should include—

◆ Pro forma income statements, month by month for the first two years, and quarterly thereafter, through all the periods covered by the plan.

◆ Pro forma income statements, month by month for the first two years, and quarterly thereafter, through all the periods covered by the plan.

◆ Pro forma cash flow, month by month for the first two years, and quarterly thereafter, through all the periods covered by the plan.

◆ A key ratios forecast, month by month for the first two years, and quarterly thereafter, through all the periods covered by the plan.

◆ Financial analysis, for a period of the first three years of the plan, using industry averages and benchmarks as supplied through reports offered through research organizations like RMA and available through most accounting firms.

*"The secret of good writing is to say an old thing in
a new way, or to say a new thing in an old way."*

Richard Harding Davis

THE COMPLETE PLAN

The supporting data exhibits, again, are composed of details on the following:

◆ Banking relationships

◆ Insurance underwriting relationships

◆ Property and equipment leases

◆ Disclosure of any and all debt contracts

◆ Documentation of any and all attendant legal matters

◆ Patent and trademark rights

◆ Full disclosure of any and all liabilities

◆ Full disclosure on any and all pending litigation or claims against the organization

◆ Details on any and all professional services providers

◆ A comprehensive risk analysis

◆ Lists of business references and any potential investors

This information is entirely optional in the operational Strategic Business Plan and is most often found in a complete strategic plan that may be made available to potential investors.

"I never know what I think about something until I read what I've written about it."

William Faulkner

ACTION INITIATORS

◆ Begin organizing your thoughts. Build an outline of the expanding level of thoughts, ideas, concepts, strategies, and actions that are accumulating in your planning efforts.
◆ Begin addressing the clear path questions in your assigned plan chapters. The questions will lead you to your destination: a finished plan.
◆ Complete your assigned plan section drafts by the agreed-upon due dates.
◆ Discipline yourself to hit your daily and weekly plan writing production goals. In general terms, depending on the number of chapters you've accepted to write, try to maintain these levels of production:

1 chapter: two to three pages per week

2 chapters: five pages per week

3 chapters: seven pages per week

4 chapters: nine pages per week

11

PUBLISH THE PLAN

"Things may come to those who wait, but only the things left by those who hustle."

Abraham Lincoln

The plan editor coordinates and drives the entire creative and production effort of the plan writing process. The plan editor coaches every section author to hit quality, quantity, and delivery marks without fail.

This editor ensures that everyone is making steady, incremental progress on schedule as the writing responsibilities travel along the production path. The plan editor calls weekly team production progress meetings, where each assigned section author offers a progress update. Following the standard small meeting format, the weekly production progress small meeting lasts about 15 to 20 minutes and uses this format—

1. Good news and progress success stories. *Inspire one another with positive evidence that you're closing in on completion, step by step.*
2. Critical numbers: How are we doing at hitting our marks? Get *updates from all section authors on where they stand in hitting their deadline commitments.*
3. Communication on important developments. *Report what is happening that might affect our progress or our process, either positively or negatively.*
4. Bottleneck/chokepoint/challenges forum. *Identify what's getting in the way for section authors and where they are encountering obstacles that may be impeding progress. Focus on solutions.*
5. Critical follow-up and corrective action commitments. *Identify and formally capture the critical follow-up and corrective ction commitments made by section authors to remain on time with their production efforts, allowing plan writing to conclude on schedule at or above established quality standards.*

This production progress meeting allows the plan editor to ensure deadlines are being met and progress is being measured. The production progress meeting keeps the importance of meeting all commitments prominent in the minds of all plan writers.

It is also the role of the plan editor to capably serve as creative coach to the selected section authors. Inevitably, even a well-meaning and self-disciplined writer will periodically hit stretches of creative cramping. He or she will hit the wall of artistic paralysis. The plan editor will serve as creative writing coach and mentor. In this essential role, the plan editor serves to assist others on the writing team when they hit creative or organizational blocks or chokepoints. The coach's responsibility is to help move past the often self-imposed limitations in creative thinking, inspiring the best efforts from each section author, clearing obstructions, and coaching to excellence.

"The art of becoming wise is the art of knowing what to overlook."

William James

FINALIZE FINANCIAL DATA

Although the plan editor need not be a financial expert, he or she must track that all necessary financial reporting forecasts and supporting financial data for the plan are being produced on schedule. The CFO or the assigned accounting team section author should attend every production progress meeting and represent the interests of the accounting department in the planning process. It is the role of the assigned accounting team leader to ensure the financial forecasts are precise and dependable. The forecasts should be checked and double-checked for accuracy, and the plausibility and viability of the assumptions underlying all of the financial data should be deeply examined, tested, and verified. When completed, the entire package of financial forecasts and supporting data should sync-up seamlessly with the overall strategies and assumptions of the entire strategic plan.

"No one will do it for you."

Ben Stein

INCORPORATE ISSUES

Each assigned key performance issues team leader must finish Hoshin key performance issues action plans, capturing detailed paths for both highlighting and tracking the execution and accomplishment of all Hoshin plan commitments. As you'll recall, these are commitments made to lead, organize, and resolve the key performance issues assignments handed out at the Strategic Planning Session. Each of the key performance issues areas was assigned a team leader; this was the person deemed most capable of addressing each of the various key performance issues identified in the strategic planning survey feedback.

This output should be delivered to the plan editor, on or before the specified due date, by each assigned key performance issues team leader in the format provided in Figures 8.3 and 8.4 found in Chapter 8.

"Good things happen to those who hustle."

Chuck Noll

COMPLETE THE STAFFING GROWTH PLANS

The annual staffing growth plans graphically show the systematic staffing growth over the term of the plan. Usually done in Microsoft's PowerPoint or an equivalent software program, it allows you to visually capture the expansion of your organization's staffing requirements. These staffing growth plans normally take the form of traditional organizational charts and cover the years comprising the strategic plan.

"The reward of a thing well done is to have it done."

Ralph Waldo Emerson

COMPILE THE FINAL PLAN DRAFT

You'll want to consciously select the appropriate look for your Strategic Business Plan. The finished document should communicate the style, philosophies, brand, and professional temperament of your organization. Generate an appropriate set of charts, graphics, tables, and illustrations to amplify the visual impact of your plan and to break up the imagery, making it more appealing to the reader.

Format the document for consistent appearance using the standard set of page editing tools accompanying your word processing software. Choose the fonts and graphic images that best communicate your organization's style, philosophies, and orientation to the markets.

Finally, to round out the final steps in preparing the strategic plan for completion and publishing, make a decision on whether or not you will include confidentiality agreements.

The confidentiality agreement is an optional but strongly advised addition to the plan documents. It is intended to lay out specific, legally binding guidelines and remedies, to protect the organization from anyone who might use your organization's plan information for dishonest or unethical purposes, or for gaining personal competitive advantages. It governs the dissemination of plan information and details solely to those selected to receive it as directed by authorized members of the leadership team.

Use the confidentiality agreement each and every time you allow someone to view the organization's strategic plan document. Do not let a copy of the plan be released to anyone without a signed confidentiality agreement. It's a good idea to keep the signed copies of the confidentiality agreement on file in a secure location. Furthermore, access to the entire strategic plan document should be restricted to only those needing full and unlimited exposure to the details of the plan. Remember that your organization has invested a considerable amount of time, capital, and creative energy into generating your strategic plan. The plan has been crafted to give you and your company a decisive and distinctive competitive advantage. Guard that investment wisely.

"The simple act of paying positive attention to people has a great deal to do with productivity."

Tom Peters

PUBLISH THE FINAL PLAN

The publishing process generally takes about a week to finalize after the actual documents for the various individual sections and supporting documents have all been completed and the final editing decisions have been made by the plan editor. Have the final version of your plan printed professionally. Print a single copy for each member of the executive leadership team and print three to five extra copies to hold in reserve for future use.

Have each member sign their copy of the confidentiality agreement to underscore the proprietary significance and nature of the plan document. For the executive leadership team, it marks the transition point to implementation.

Now that you're moving into the implementation phase of the strategic planning process and are sharing the entire plan among only a select group of recipients, you may want to consider breaking out the plan's executive summary into a shortened version of the larger strategic plan. This will allow you to share it with your entire staff, bringing them into a working awareness of the organization's strategic direction, without giving away the more proprietary strategic details of the entire plan. This assures a greater level buy-in and commitment from your staff and allows for a greater measure of control over who has knowledge of the entire plan details. Even in this abridged and abbreviated internal executive summary, it is important to stress the confidential nature of the information contained in the document. It's not a bad idea to have everyone who receives the executive summary also sign a confidentiality agreement to emphasize the proprietary value of the document and the powerful value it contains.

You can also use the shortened executive summary version as a recruiting tool. On a selective basis, it is best shared with *only* those strongest final candidates who have passed rigorous screening. For these kinds of desired candidates, the executive summary version of the plan can be a very encouraging inside look at where your organization is headed. It can reinforce positive perceptions about your organization in the mind of your candidate and can create potent awareness as to how confident and organized you are in approaching future opportunities. It signals you are a reasonably open organization and implies you are feeling comfortable enough with the candidate to trust them with some sensitive and proprietary information about your company. Again, get a signed confidentiality agreement. Using your executive summary in acquiring "A" level talent could make a major difference in the performance of your organization.

"The older I get, the more wisdom I find in the ancient rule of taking first things first, a process which often reduces the most complex human problem to a manageable proportion."

Dwight D. Eisenhower

ACTION INITIATORS

- The plan editor coordinates and drives the plan production process.
- The plan editor schedules and convenes weekly production progress meetings with all plan section authors.
- The plan editor serves as creative coach and mentor during the plan writing process.
- The plan editor ensures that all financial forecasts and supporting data are completed and accurate and in sync with plan strategies.
- Hoshin action plans are assembled in narrative format, using the suggested methods and processes.
- Staffing growth plans are completed for the period covered by the plan.
- Compile, format, and edit all sections of the final plan draft.
- Publish the final plan.
- Issue numbered plan copies to all appropriate members of the leadership team. Obtain signed confidentiality agreements from each recipient.
- Create a secure and sanitized version of the executive summary to share with staff and with high-caliber candidates being recruited to join the organization.

12

EXECUTE THE PLAN

*"Good ideas are not adopted automatically. They must
be driven into practice with courageous patience."*

Admiral Hyman Rickover

There is no reason to wait until the entire plan is completed to begin putting selected portions of the plan into immediate motion. From the moment you complete the owner's vision, begin executing your quickly solidifying vision. Deploy your attention, your resources, and your full team immediately in pursuit of your emerging short-term top 5 and first of 5 goals.

"Action springs not from thought, but from a readiness for responsibility."

Dietrich Bonhoeffer

TAKE ACTION

After the plan has been shared with your organization's leaders and everyone is clear on their respective roles and accountabilities for executing the plan, it's time to get started. Although there are highly unusual and completely unanticipated situations that could come along and force you to rethink the plan's fundamental premises, such earth-shaking events are rare. The above-average strategic plan can be implemented forcefully, without the need for perpetual bouts of second-guessing. If the initial premises were sound and if the strategies evolving from those premises remain valid, do not hesitate a moment in vigorously applying the full talents and energies of your team in driving the plan forward.

"Procrastination is opportunity's natural assassin."

Victor Kiam

SET BENCHMARKS

Benchmarking permits an organization to recognize opportunities for improvement during the early stages of implementing the Strategic Business Plan. Benchmarking establishes the best levels of performance being realized within an industry. To establish benchmarks, look for industry leaders who are top performers in the areas you are trying to improve. Benchmarks provide a reality check of how you are performing against others in your industry. Benchmarking raises the bar on performance and forces an organization to self-arrest before it is lulled into a comfort zone of complacency and mediocrity.

"If everything's under control, you're going too slow."

Mario Andretti

Effective benchmarking is objective, purposeful, driven by critical numbers measurement, rigorously information-intensive, and action-oriented. The benchmarks for plan implementation, in this application, are the top 5 and first of 5 goals for the organization that back up the plan in the short, intermediate, and long term, forming the mileposts by which we track and measure our plan progress. Progress is also measured in the Hoshin action plan performance, in how well actual progress is tracking against the individual key performance issues goals.

"You prove your worth with your actions, not with your mouth."

Pat Riley

MEASURE PROGRESS

The progress of plan execution is measured in different ways and occurs at different times following plan completion. The plan needs to remain prominent in the minds of all team members. People need a heightened awareness that progress is being tracked, reported, and evaluated by the leadership team. Those responsible to advance their action plan accountabilities to the results stage need to know what is expected of them in terms of performance. They must all be aware that their timely delivery of the expected results is imperative to continue forward progress.

An elementary opportunity to assess and communicate plan progress occurs at the departmental level during the weekly, monthly, and quarterly departmental team meetings. Departmental leaders have the responsibility to keep their teams attentive to the demands and the schedules of their respective key performance action plan commitments. Department leaders should make a habit of spotlighting one or two goals at each meeting. Make a point of letting the teams know that staying on schedule is important in advancing plan output.

The majority of the formal tracking, reporting, and evaluation of strategic plan progress takes place during the monthly and quarterly executive leadership team meetings. A permanent agenda item during these sessions is the comparison of forecast plan performance with actual plan performance. Each department leader is expected to provide an update to the entire leadership team on advances they have initiated or completed since the last periodic review. The value of using the monthly and quarterly executive team meetings to assess the execution and implementation progress of the strategic plan scrves as an early warning system to alert top leadership to challenges or obstacles in the way of sustaining acceptable levels of advancement. The meetings also allow leadership to make necessary mid-course corrections well before smaller problems become systemic and destructive.

Another, more formal opportunity for review occurs during the annual strategic planning update meeting. Usually held in the ninth or tenth month of an organization's fiscal year, this is when the leadership team meets to evaluate progress from the year just passed. The team will consider making adjustments to the plan, changes in the business model, changes in the markets served, changes in the customer base, or any other substantive changes affecting the ongoing viability of assumptions at the heart of the original Strategic Business Plan. It is an opportunity to take the pulse of the team and examine their belief and commitment levels of the directions the original plan advocated.

"Success seems to be connected to action. Successful people
keep moving. They make mistakes, but they don't quit."

Conrad Hilton

Right now your strategic planning success hangs in the balance, dependent on the quality of your elite team and on your brand of leadership to effectively execute the abundant, complex, detailed actions required to deliver the outcomes you seek.

ACTION INITIATORS

- ◆ Begin implementing your strategic plan immediately after the Strategic Planning Session. Do not wait for the plan to be completed.
- ◆ After the plan is completed, ramp up your implementation and execution of the plan aggressively.
- ◆ Establish benchmarks for measuring and marking plan implementation and execution progress.
- ◆ Use the weekly, monthly, and quarterly meetings as opportunities to track, report, evaluate, and communicate plan progress.
- ◆ Use the annual strategic planning update meeting to evaluate and adjust the continuing viability of all plan aspects.
- ◆ Lead the execution and implementation of all strategic plan actions "from the front."

13

MONITOR RESULTS

"Great is the art of beginning, but greater is the art of ending."
Henry Wadsworth Longfellow

To be both prudent and realistic, it is a good thing for you to periodically re-examine the plan at several important points in time. The first full year of a new plan, you should review the plan on a quarterly basis, and the best place and time to do so is during the quarterly meetings of the executive leadership team.

ANNUAL PLAN REVIEW

The fourth quarterly meeting should be your organization's annual meeting, coinciding with when you begin your annual budgeting cycle. During each of these quarterly sessions, and most importantly during the annual meeting, you should examine your major strategic themes along with their respective linked activities.

◆ Have they all withstood the initial tests of implementation and execution?

◆ What have you learned during the quarter and the year-to-date?

◆ What adjustments do you need to make?

◆ Are you on track or off track with your plan forecasts?

◆ Is the plan providing the desired results? If not, what should you do to either re-align or re-direct your organization's efforts back on track with the plan?

"You either make dust or you eat dust."
H. Jackson Brown Jr.

Ask these questions at each of the individual quarterly meetings. At the annual meeting, devote a full day exclusively to examining, updating, validating, and reaffirming the strategic plan. You should plan on reviewing and updating your vision at the annual meeting.

◆ Has the vision shifted in the preceding 12 months?

◆ Have new realities emerged to alter earlier assumptions or forecasts?

◆ Have any of the needs of key players altered in any ways?

◆ Has the competitive landscape changed in any significant or troublesome ways?

◆ Should you modify your game plan from an offensive to a defensive strategy, or vice versa?

◆ Should you continue on the path you've outlined for your organization because it was originally sound and well-conceived and is still valid in virtually every aspect?

These are the kinds of questions to pose to yourself and your leadership team during your annual meeting.

> *"The man who gets the most satisfactory results is not always the man with the most brilliant single mind, but rather the man who can best coordinate the brains and talents of his associates."*
>
> *W. Alton Jones*

ADJUST THE PLAN

Rest assured that the very moment you get comfortable believing you've got a masterful and bullet-proof strategic plan, one that will generate decisive and enduring competitive advantages, is precisely when something will go wrong.

Changes will inevitably occur in even the most carefully constructed and conservative of strategic planning processes. To save yourself from the dangers of rigid or erroneous strategies and operational processes based on misinterpretations of facts and data, it is vitally important for you and your fellow leaders to remain open, flexible, and adaptive to changing conditions.

In the ladder of inference, awareness of the various "rungs" on the ladder—observing data, adding our own meaning, drawing conclusions, creating stories, and establishing beliefs—allows us to check off our perceptions against more objective realities.

> *"Let me tell you the secret that has led me to my goal: My strength lies solely in my tenacity."*
>
> *Louis Pasteur*

FIGURE 13.1—THE LADDER OF INFERENCE

Establish Beliefs	
Create Stories	
Draw Conclusions	
Add Own Meaning	
Observe Data	
Living	

ASSESS PROGRESS

Revisit your Current Reality Assessment at least once a year and re-administer it, either to yourself or to your entire executive leadership team. Use your first Current Reality Assessment as your foundation for feedback, as your point of departure in this process. It will provide the original set of marks—the benchmarks—for gauging progress. Keep in mind that the Current Reality Assessment is a subjective instrument. As such, it is no less important to realize that it is a powerful tool for measuring perceptions and for identifying shifts in perception over time.

Use the Current Reality Assessment to take the pulse of yourself and your organization. What it becomes is the annual physical checkup of your organization and each key leader.

◆ Do you perceive to be making progress since your last checkup?

◆ Where have your perceptions changed, and why?

◆ Where are you better off *today* than you considered yourself at the previous checkup point?

◆ Where might you be backsliding, and why?

Give yourself a thorough, introspective evaluation. Have others in the organization participate and do the same. Compare notes and perceptions. This evaluation provides an invigorating opportunity for healthy, even heated discussions about your organization's state. Where there is disagreement, seek convergence of the varied perceptions so that everyone has a commonly agreed-upon set of perceptions of your organization's current realities. Seek alignment on the updated current key performance issues facing the company. Decide concordantly on what needs attention, both as a unified team *and* as a cohesive organization.

"One thought driven home is better than three left on base."

James Liter

SHARE PROGRESS

After you've completed your first Strategic Business Plan, you'll discover that updating your current realities, your vision, and the strategic plan itself on an annual basis gets much easier than when you did it the first time. Updating and refining an established business plan requires much less effort than was originally invested in producing your very first plan. Updating your vision and your plan, following the annual meeting, should require no more than a day of concentrated effort.

After you've updated your current realities, your vision, and your strategic plan following the annual meeting, gather the entire organization together for the annual organizational meeting. This provides the opportunity to update everyone on the progress made in the preceding 12 months in implementing and executing the Strategic Business Plan. Address any shortfalls, highlight all emerging challenges, illuminate any noteworthy movements in operational direction or strategic thinking, and clarify any modifications of course, goals, tactics, activities, or organizational emphasis. The annual organizational meeting also affords leadership the opening to enlist new or renewed levels of commitment from staff, to effectively tackle the next rounds of tests facing the organization as it continues to evolve in the ongoing growth of the strategic plan.

"Don't tell me how hard you work. Tell me how much you get done."

James Ling

The annual meeting also gives you and your executive leadership team the chance to tap into the perceptions and opinions of your entire staff. Solicit feedback. Ask questions.

◆ How do *you* think you're doing?

◆ Are you feeling better *today* than you were a year ago about the organization and your role in it? Why or why not?

◆ Are there any issues important to you that we are not addressing at this time? If so, what are they?

As an added measure, allow your staff the opportunity to influence your perceptions through the annual staff survey. Remember that self-awareness is the foundation for moving to meaningful results.

◆ Are there any surprises out there?

◆ Do you have an accurate read on the mood of your organization? How is morale?

◆ Are there any fresh new ideas on how to increase revenues, profitability, or cash flow?

◆ Are there any ways to make their jobs easier and to make the organization more productive?

Take the opportunity to formally take the pulse of your organization through the medium of the annual survey. Properly administered, it will deliver a treasure of awareness to you and your fellow decision makers. The feedback will include priceless gems that will allow you to make better decisions along the path to your vision and to convert current realities into the dreams you have for yourself and your organization.

"Do, or do not. There is no 'try'"

Yoda, Jedi Master

ACTION INITIATORS

◆ Review and update your Strategic Business Plan at the quarterly meetings for your executive leadership team.
◆ Conduct a comprehensive review and analysis of your plan at the annual meeting, taking a full day to re-examine your themes, linked actions, forecasts, and underlying assumptions.
◆ Revise the plan as significant changes occur and require adjustments.
◆ Conduct a current realities update on an annual basis.
◆ Consider conducting an annual survey of your staff, to update your levels of awareness of the mood, morale, and ideas of your organization in improving commitment and performance levels.
◆ Hold an annual organizational meeting to communicate updates on the strategic plan and to open up a dialog with your staff on strategic or operational issues.
◆ Make a decision, and a commitment, as to whether you will commit time, attention, creative energies, and the resources of your organization to creating an effective Strategic Business Plan.

RESOURCES

Mastering the Rockefeller Habits
By Verne Harnish
Copyright © 2002 by Verne Harnish
Publisher:
SelectBooks, Inc.
Mr. Kenzi Sugihara, President
New York, NY
(212) 759-4428
www.selectbooks.com

The Successful Business Plan: Secrets & Strategies
By Rhonda M. Abrams
Copyright © 1991, 1993 by Rhonda M. Abrams
Publisher:
The Oasis Press
Publishing Services, Inc. (PSI, Inc.)
PSI Research
300 North Valley Drive
Grants Pass, OR 97526
(541) 479-9464
www.psi-research.com

The Quantum Leap Strategy
By Price Pritchett
Copyright © 1991 by Price Pritchett, Ph.D.
Publisher:
Pritchett & Associates, Inc./Pritchett LLC
5800 Granite Parkway, Suite 450
Plano, TX 75024
(972) 731-1500
www.pritchettnet.com

Obsessions of an Extraordinary Executive
By Patrick Lencioni
Copyright © 2000 by Jossey-Bass Inc.
Publisher:
Jossey-Bass Inc.
350 Sansome Street
San Francisco, CA 94104
(888) 378-2537
www.josseybass.com

Verne Harnish
President
Gazelles, Inc.
21246 Dubois Court
Ashburn, VA 20147
(703) 858-2400

The Five Temptations of a CEO
By Patrick Lencioni
Copyright © 1998 by Jossey-Bass Inc.
Publisher:
Jossey-Bass Inc.
350 Sansome Street
San Francisco, CA 94104
(888) 378-2537
www.josseybass.com

Mr. Patrick Lencioni
President
The Table Group, Inc.
6400 Hollis Street, Suite 5
Emeryville, CA 94608
(510) 596-9292

Smart Moves for People In Charge
By Sam Deep and Lyle Sussman
Copyright © 1995 by Sam Deep and Lyle Sussman
Publisher:
Addison-Wesley
75 Arlington Street, Suite 300;
Boston, MA 02116
(617) 848-6000
www.aw.com

Mr. Sam Deep
1920 Woodside Road
Glenshaw, PA 15116
(412) 487-2379

Successful Executive's Handbook
By Susan H. Gebelein, David G. Lee, Kristie J. Nelson-Neuhaus, and Elaine B. Sloan
2000 Edition; Copyright © 1996, 1999 by Personnel Decisions International Corp.
Publisher:
Personnel Decisions International Corp.
2000 Plaza VII Tower
45 South Seventh Street
Minneapolis, MN 55402-1608
(800) 633-4410
www.personneldecisions.com

Beware the Naked Man Who Offers You His Shirt
By Harvey Mackay
Copyright © 1990 by Harvey Mackay
Publisher:
William Morrow and Company
105 Madison Avenue
New York, NY 10016
c/o www.harpercollins.com

Permissions Department
HarperCollins Books
1350 Avenue of the Americas
New York, NY 10019
(212) 261-6500

Handbook of Business Planning
By JIAN Tools For Sales, Inc.
Copyright © 1988-2000 by JIAN, Inc.
Publisher:
JIAN, Inc.
1975 West El Camino Real
Mountain View, CA 94040
(650) 254-5600
(800) 346-5426
www.jian.com

Creating and Implementing Your Strategic Plan
By John M. Bryson and Farnum K. Alston
Copyright © 1996 by Jossey-Bass, Inc.
Publisher:
Jossey-Bass Inc.
350 Sansome Street
San Francisco, CA 94104
(888) 378-2537
www.josseybass.com

Execution: The Discipline of Getting Things Done
By Larry Bossidy and Ram Charan
Copyright © 2002 by Larry Bossidy and Ram Charan
Publisher:
Crown Business
Crown Publishing Group and Three Rivers Press
2633 Lincoln Boulevard, # 407
Santa Monica, CA 90405
(310) 842-4882
www.crownbusiness.com

Random House, Inc.
1540 Broadway
New York, NY 10036
(212) 782-9000

For books published by the Crown Trade group:

Copyright Department
Random House, Inc.
299 Park Avenue
New York, NY 10171